# THE NANOSECOND NETWORLDERS

## CHANGING LIVES IN AN INSTANT... FOREVER

### A Modern Business Fairytale

BY MELISSA GIOVAGNOLI
AND DAVID R. STOVER

# The Nanosecond Networlders –

## Changing Lives in an Instant... Forever

**A Modern Business Fairytale**

**By Melissa Giovagnoli
and David R. Stover**

# ABOUT THE AUTHORS

**Melissa Giovagnoli -**
Melissa Giovagnoli is the author and/or co-author of seven top-selling books and one of the world's leading experts on the development of individual and community networks that focus on socially responsible business growth as a means of growing brand loyalty and developing internal (employee) and external (customer) community networks. For fifteen years she has been involved in cause-related marketing and leadership programs
Melissa is the president of Networlding, a learning organization focused on helping individuals build trusting, satisfying and empowering relationships faster to grow their organizations, businesses or careers through the creation of transformational opportunities. She has been a guest on both radio and television including *The Today Show, CNN, WGN, CNBC* and *FOX*. One of her books was featured on *The Oprah Winfrey Show*. She is a frequent presenter at conferences looking for interactive sessions.

**David R. Stover -**
David Stover has spent the last fifteen years searching for the 'silver bullet' in business consulting, not expecting to find it, but enjoying the search nonetheless. In addition to consulting with many of the world's largest companies in Europe, Asia, and the Americas, Mr. Stover has helped launch a myriad of new businesses, many of them outside the USA. He focuses on new and innovative ways in which companies can leverage competencies to transform themselves and improve their performance.
He specializes in Consumer Innovation and is a frequent speaker at industry, technology and emerging business conferences. He has led practices in Iberia, the UK, and the USA, and worked in over 18 countries. His creative leadership style along with his awareness of the values of the cultures in which he works has led to programs of significant, sustainable value. This is Mr. Stover's first book working in collaboration with Ms. Giovagnoli.

For more information about Networlding, go to www.networlding.com

# Contents

*"It is as hard to tell the truth as it is to hide it."*
Baltasar Gracian, Spanish Writer, 1648

# CHAPTER 1
## Once upon a Time…

Once upon a time, not so long ago, there was a great adventure…

That's how most fairytales start. But this tale of Darryl and Marie's isn't a fantasy with the locked tower-princess and the white knight on a noble steed seeking her freedom. This also isn't one of those modern-day adventures that begins benignly, highlights the cleverness of the main characters and the ineptitude of their adversaries, and then ends with the hero and heroine retiring to the countryside with victory in hand and their stock options intact.

This adventure, like most day-to-day real life adventures, has a little of this, a little of that. It takes place in the world of ideas as much as in the world of acts. It takes place in small towns, in large cities, in America and abroad. It takes place in the boardroom and the bedroom (no, this is not THAT kind of book!). As is typical of real-life adventures, the people in it don't realize they are in an adventure until it's far too late to get out. And just like in real life, there aren't only the good and the bad, or the wise and the ignorant, but also the right and the wrong. And sometimes the good guys do the wrong things and the bad guys do the right things…after all…that's real life, right?

Who are Darryl and Marie? Why, they are you and me. And the obvious differences are not nearly as important as the obvious similarities – similarities in everything they do and learn and grow into and everything we do and learn and grow into on our journey through our careers, our families, and ourselves.

**"'Capitalism and Altruism are incompatible…capitalism and altruism cannot coexist in man or the same society.'"**

Darryl read the Ayn Rand quote aloud and sat back with a puzzled look. He carefully turned over the tattered old copy of *Time* Magazine and looked at the date on the cover: February 29, 1960.

He coughed and shifted his cross-legged position to be more comfortable in the dusty attic of this old chalet he'd rented for the month. As he looked at the 1960 date on the magazine's cover, he thought that this 'thing' he'd been feeling about his career had been long at work in the fabric of the country, if Rand was to be believed.

He remembered reading *The Fountainhead* and *Atlas Shrugged* as a teenager. And like everyone else, he'd walked around for weeks with ideas whirling about the freedom that Rand promised with her rationalistic value system. He'd heard her called a philosopher, not a writer, but he never really looked into her philosophy. If the last thirty years of American business were any testament, he'd have to say that a lot of people had read her books but looked into her philosophy and adopted her model more passionately than he.

He looked around the dim attic at dusty boxes over-filled with old books, half-repaired chairs, and piles upon piles of dated magazines…some French, German, English. It was the second week of his holiday respite, and as usual, after seven days of sleeping and walking the cool mountain countryside of springtime Spain, he was getting restless. In his early years working in the States he rarely managed to get a vacation of more than a week. More often he grabbed four-day weekends between projects and occasionally went home before seven p.m. – considering the evening a day off. New economy, old economy...it was all the same when you were building a career.

Over the last few years Darryl had awakened more and more to the necessity of recharging his batteries. Unfortunately, his American employer didn't feel the same way, so there was a constant battle to get the time he needed to recharge. A couple of overseas assignments in his twenty years had lent further impetus to August being the month, if at all possible, to take off. Of course, in his line of work, that meant crazy hours in July and more crazy hours in September, but the trade-off seemed reasonable. After all, he worked crazy hours anyway.

When he'd drifted up to the third floor of this house after a large cup of coffee and a quick read of the paper, he'd been immediately intrigued by the thick door leading to another staircase at the back of the home. With just a bit of nervousness, he pressed open the door and mounted the stairs to find himself surrounded by a reader's heaven in old books and magazines. He'd stayed in the attic more than two hours sifting through boxes, exploring, when he came across the old copy of *Time* Magazine and read the article from start to finish.

He rose stiffly to his feet, and ducking his head to avoid the low ceiling, made his way around the boxes to the doorway, still clutching the magazine in his hand. Downstairs, he poured himself another cup of coffee and sat back in the chair. What was it that made him feel so unfulfilled? His career, on the surface, was fine. He was a high-energy global consultant with enough clients and work to keep him blissfully busy for the next ten years. He had many acquaintances, a few good friends, and lots of phone numbers in his palm pilot. But something was missing, and this article really brought it into focus.

He always had a more personal style to selling and doing consulting work than others. Even with all the technology and methodology in the world, he'd always just cut to the core when discussing services with CEO's. Regardless of whether he was selling work or executing it he wanted to connect on a personal level with the people he was helping.

Unfortunately, many executives were uncomfortable with this approach. They preferred a less personal, more analytical discussion of the issues. Darryl wondered now if they were afraid that their judgement would be impaired if they had a personal connection with their consultant. In the end, most preferred to keep the conversations devoid of relationship, centered on the facts. But what were those facts that would help a business be successful in this new, ultra-networked world? How do you merge companies or build more valuable strategic alliances or establish key partnerships that complement your own business model? How do you break down silos and get employees and divisions to work together more effectively? How do you build truly customer-centric organizations? How could capitalism and altruism co-exist?

Darryl experienced many times in a new business relationship that when he put his client's interests above his own he benefited just as much or more in the end. There had recently been a marketing executive who had shared some concerns over his marketing plan for the coming year. Even though it was not part of the scope of his current project with that client, and Darryl didn't charge any fees for his time, he spent many evenings and a few weekends working with that executive to finalize the marketing plan. His personal investment, made with no expectation of any direct reward, resulted in the client retaining Darryl's company as one of their preferred service providers. He was pleased that the executive recognized his personal investment, but Darryl hadn't had any preconceived plan for the result that he achieved. He had merely been operating from an unselfish desire to help.

He was convinced that connecting 'altruistically' with his clients enabled him to more effectively serve them. He believed that if the consulting process started antiseptically more times than not it would end that way; and a lot of holes would be left along the way. Talented people would be left behind and good market opportunities would be missed. He'd seen it.

As he sat thinking about the Rand article, he realized clearly that he was at a crossroads with his career. He had worked his whole life in environments that didn't support his personal philosophy of relationship building. He felt good about going out of his way for others when he felt he could offer assistance and add value. He enjoyed the feeling of connectedness that resulted from assisting in an opportunity where he felt he could be of value.

Yet, everyone he knew had a plethora of phone numbers and associates they could call and connect with when they needed to generate new opportunities for their business. But these approaches seemed only sporadically successful. They were not based on any pre-developed relationships of value, but were opportunistic in nature. Whether the personal connection was made to begin the selling process, to inquire as to employment, or to manage a department, people tended to divide into those sincerely interested in building relationships first and those who were simply latching onto a relationship when it would further their own ambitions.

Because he was tired of working with people who manipulated relationships whenever they smelled the first scent of opportunity, Darryl was becoming more and more burnt out as the years went by. He realized that unless he was able to find people to work with that held similar values, he was going to continue to be frustrated. Deep down, he knew there was way for him to do business the way he liked and felt was more effective. The run-in he'd had with his North American leadership team on the day before he was to leave on his holiday still stung at his memory. He took a sip of his coffee, ran his long fingers through his hair, and replayed in his mind the discussion he'd had in Chicago.

✳

"Well, what do you think, Darryl?" The tone was gruff, although the older partner's countenance was curious.

It was a late Friday afternoon and the short spring Chicago days were just beginning to stretch beyond the evening rush hour. Low sunlight slipped through the slatted windows and played a pattern on the far wall behind Darryl's head. He was

5

weary from a long week of work on both American coasts and was still suffering from a four-country workout the prior week in which he ate most of his meals on either airplanes or in his hotel room, while spending his days visiting key accounts in Europe.

He looked up from the binder in front of him and surveyed the room. It was filled with heavy unit partners (HUP's) who all had a stake in the status quo of the global consulting firm's current industry and services alignment. They had just been discussing a business study in which some of them would be required to give up their 'service lines' and merge operations in order to improve the company's effectiveness at handling global clients. Darryl had been asked to review the plan, which another consulting company prepared, and provide his point-of-view. He took a deep breath.

"Carpe diem," he said. There was a rustle about the room as bodies shifted and papers rustled.

"What was that?" came a voice from some unknown source in the room.

"Seize the day," Darryl said again. He stood up, a statement itself in that room of infamous posturers, presenters, and pontificators. He looked across the room and saw the perfect ties, the Hugo Boss suits, the silver rings, the cuffed shirts, the monogrammed pens hovering over blank sheets of crisp, lined notebooks. Inside he cringed. 'But for the grace of God…' he thought, and then smiled to himself. But for the grace of God he could end up like them, but he had continued to change over the years while they had not. Into what he was changing into, he did not know. But he did recognize a change in himself that was gathering steam.

He gathered his thoughts together and started to speak. "On the surface, the answer is simple: you should accept the changes if they add value to the firm; you should reject them if they don't." He looked around the room quietly.

It didn't show, but he was a little on the edge. Usually he was on-point, fired up on caffeine and adrenaline, and since he'd been working so much in Europe lately, nicotine. Boardroom meetings on two hours of sleep after a ten-hour flight were normal. This group wasn't any more impressive than the dozens of CEOs and Chairmans he'd faced in the previous decade on his own.

Being a partner in a growing consultancy created numerous opportunities for the entrepreneurial side of him to shine. Not that anyone within the firm ever saw the light or understood the nature of its luminosity, but that was okay. His clients saw it. The only added element with today's group from the many he'd faced before was that most of these gentlemen paid his salary. He grinned to himself. Money didn't motivate him, much. After a few years in business (he'd originally dreamed of being a poor starving artist) he'd escaped the financial and other dependencies that led so many of his peers to accept boring staff jobs working for despotic bosses in value-eroding enterprises.

He'd used his career to explore and to learn more about people…and himself. Today, he felt a rising energy that always preceded his best efforts. There was no fear. There was no hesitation. He was ready to deliver. He breathed carefully in and began to speak.

"I've read the same reports you have," he said. "And I've grown up in this company the same way you have." He saw nodding heads affirm his statement. "And one thing I know for sure is that our clients time after time say privately that 'change is change for the worse' even while publicly they claim that they are 'agents of change' in their own companies. We've all seen it. And some of our toughest assignments have come from misreading the board or the executive team and believing what they say, not what they do. Well, I think its time for us to do, to practice what we teach.

"Do I want this re-alignment? This change? On one hand, I do. Intellectually, I realize that in order for us to provide world-class services, we need to line up with our clients differently than we have in the past. In order to provide world-class value we need to think differently about how we work with our clients, about how we organize ourselves to respond to their needs, about how we measure our own success along with theirs.

"On the other hand, I don't like it. I like the way things are. Gene and I," Darryl nodded towards an executive dressed more casually than the rest sitting at the far end of the table, quietly sipping his afternoon coffee, but looking sharply attentive, "Gene and I have worked our industry model to perfection in North American, Iberia, and the UK. We've leveraged the American expertise in third generation eTechnologies and multi-channel business models and done an excellent job working with some of the powerhouses in Europe to put them on the map in their own markets. More than anything, I think our approach to building and maintaining relationships based on common 'values' not just common 'goals' has been a linchpin in our success. You've heard me speak many times on the need for us to create a more proactive, network environment to share ideas, connect with our clients, and adapt to the changing business communities we face out there.

"This plan," said Darryl waving to the report in front of them all, "represents the foundations of a business change that will help us to do more effectively what the best of us do already. And particularly with the industries converging as they are, it's even more vital for us to create a sustainable set of relationships and 'access points' to the executive suites of our clients across industries in order to continue to grow this company.

"I know we have to change. If our clients reorganize every four or five years, switching out CEOs and CIOs and CMOs etc., then how can we continue to bring relevant messages to them, continue to connect with big ideas if we do less?" He looked about the room quizzically.

"If anything, we need to reorganize and reinvent our thinking, and if necessary our organizations every eighteen months or so just to stay ahead of our clients and anticipate their needs. This issue of industry convergence (i.e., energy companies selling merchandise, retailers selling telecom services, etc.) is serious. This issue of moving away from 'transaction-oriented' networking to 'value-oriented' relationships is serious. I think we need to adapt to a spaghetti bowl of business models and a spaghetti bowl of client service values much different from the SIC-code based industry definitions of twenty years ago that we are still using.

"This change is long overdue. And though I personally might object to half a dozen minor points about the plan, I can't object to its intention, which is to position us to continue to grow and continue to stay one step ahead of our clients." Darryl took a sip of water before continuing.

"I know this is difficult for some of us in the room. Some of you have spent your lives developing relationships in your industries and are well known because of it. You've helped drive our business into the multi-billions. And you wonder how in the world your best and prime clients can be served under new partners, new messages, or new organizations. You wonder about the potential impact to our reputation, and to your reputations, if the partners in the reorganized firm don't provide them with the expertise, the experience, the 'smarts' that you've provided for all these years." Darryl paused to take a breath. "I say that it's precisely because you are worried that we will succeed."

His words caused a stir amongst the executives, but Darryl continued. "If you weren't worried, then I would be. Extreme confidence is a mask for either incompetence or ignorance, and no one in this room qualifies as either. So what is my recommendation? As I said before, Carpe Diem. Seize the day. Let's do it. Let's make a commitment to recognize, own, and leverage from our personal and professional values and not accept anything less than this same commitment from all those stakeholders we serve. And I'd further propose that we don't even go through the few points of concern I do have or the numerous challenges each and every one of you have. I say, it feels right. Call it emotional intelligence or just Darryl's executive recommendation. Any way you slice it, I say it's the right thing to do. I'd adopt the program 'as is'. Announce the changes tomorrow, and let the new leaders of our converged practice lines work out the adjustments instead of having us do it in this room today."

An even greater stir in the room ensued. Darryl saw heads shaking back and forth, pens scratching on notepads, a general restlessness. A tremor of concern rippled through him. Perhaps he'd misjudged the leadership qualities of his executive team. Nothing breeds failure like success, he knew. Success creates blind spots, boosts egos, calcifies reflexes. He hoped they weren't so ingrained in their past success that they couldn't see the necessity for changes today.

He wrapped up his comments. "So you ask what I think? I think that the new leadership partners, with your help as executive coaches and serving as a 'council' of advisors, will have the energy and market focus to take the best of our past, merge it with the best of today, and create tremendous opportunities for our company in the near future." With that, Darryl re-seated himself.

A few low conversations occurred in various spots around the table that Darryl's ears couldn't pick up. He wasn't sure where this discussion would go next. The chairman, looking like the well-fit retired colonel in his tailored suit that he was, looked around the table, got a few nods of acquiescence, and stood up.

"Thank you, Darryl. We know you have some last minute client activities that you need to take care of before heading off on your 'extended' holiday." There was a series of muffled smiles about the room and Darryl grimaced slightly. This American-based organization still didn't understand the value of refreshing their thinking with extended time off like the Europeans. A four-day weekend five or six times a year was the proud legacy of most of these executives. Little did they know that lack of perspective and lack of outside stimulus led to slower market reactions, increased calcification of decision making, etc. The chairman continued. "We appreciate your candor. We also appreciate you coming down today to share your insights with us. You know we all value your perspective and your 'outside-in' thinking greatly. Thanks again."

Darryl rose from his chair, collected his notes, and with a small smile of appreciation made his way to the double-door exit. As the doors closed behind him, he heard the heated debate begin.

A few hours later, as he was cleaning up the last item on his to do list and preparing to head to the airport, a head popped into his office. It was Gene. Gene glanced quickly about the office, noting Darryl's movements with keen insight.

"How you doing, buddy?" Gene asked as he slipped quietly into chair in front of Darryl's desk. Darryl looked at him as he continued to pack away the last of his papers. The look on Gene's face told him enough. He snapped his bag closed and walked around the side of his desk, heading for the door.

"They voted it down, didn't they?" he replied to Gene, ignoring his question and asking his own.

"Yep." Gene's slight southern accent became more pronounced when he was distressed, and Darryl could distinctly hear the drawl as he rounded his desk and reached out his hand to shake Gene's.

"Well, I've helped a lot of dinosaur companies turn things around. I just never thought I'd be working for one." The note of disgust in Darryl's voice was unmistakable.

"Now, Darryl," began Gene, drawling out his words even more, "you have to understand that most of these boys haven't been in the market much in the last few years, too much administering the business to spend time in front of clients. So you and I both know that 'them dogs can't hunt anymore' so to speak. Understand that they just don't see things the same way as you and I do. And as for that consulting report? Well, you know as well as I do that consultants are the worst clients because they think they know everything. So did you really expect us to take that report and believe every word of it when it was created by a firm that didn't even exist at a time when we were already over $1 Billion in fees?"

"What difference does that make?" exclaimed a frustrated Darryl. "A drunk on the street can tell you that the sun rises in the east. Lack of general credibility has nothing to do with whether something is specifically true or not! If we start believing things based solely on the source and not on our own business judgement and experience, what and who are we to believe?"

Darryl reached the door and turned around to speak to his oldest friend. "Gene, you and I both know that this is the right thing for the firm to do. If we couldn't convince our leadership team of that objective truth, then I don't have anything else to say." With that, Darryl moved quickly through the door, out of the office, and into the waiting car curbside to take him to the airport, leaving a pained look on his friend Gene's face.

✳

The sun had long ago descended behind the mountains to the west that lay between Segovia and Madrid. Night had settled on the hillside around Darryl's chalet like a thick wool blanket. Brilliant stars lit the theatre overhead, and Darryl took a last deep breath as he stepped back inside his doorway.

He looked around the small confines of the chalet. Hardwood floors, tiny kitchen appliances, narrow windows. It was perfect. He felt far, far removed from the antiseptic world of modern business. He felt far removed from the results of that last meeting in Chicago, although it still bothered him immensely. This holiday respite felt charged with something different. He felt it. Whether it was the Rand article, the sweetness of the Spanish air, or the poignancy of the meeting in Chicago, he felt that in the next few weeks while he relaxed and regenerated he was going to reach some conclusions about his life. He had known even during the Chicago meeting, reflecting upon his peers and bosses in the room, that he some time ago had set off into uncharted waters and didn't know where or how it would all end.

He laid himself down on the sofa in the living room and picked up the latest book he was reading. Isabel Allende was a magnificent writer. Her words painted a lush tapestry of the mystic and mundane as she explored the hopes and horrors of 19th century Chile. Darryl felt her soul reflected in the words sculpted on the pages before him. She was the perfect compliment, in her intimate portrait of her Chilean characters, to the richness and humanity he always felt when resting in Spain and that he always lacked when he was in the States. He was deep into his book when there was a sudden knock at the door.

※

*"True genius is holding two seemingly diametrically opposed ideas in your mind at the same time"*.
Albert Einstein

# CHAPTER 2
## Marie's Conflict

Marie was not always this unhappy.

In the last few months there had been several times when she actually enjoyed what she was doing at the telecommunications company where she worked. She was pleased, for instance, by her staff's enthusiasm over the launch of a new channel in Madrid. She particularly liked the idea of selling cell phones at coffee shops where she could see her company's customers buying espressos and cappuccinos with more cell time or new cell accessories.

The proliferation of cellular technology into all walks of life in Europe was far more than the United States. Marie was ecstatic about getting access to that huge consumer base and all the creative applications companies had already been applying cellular technologies to, from vending machine purchases to train tickets and merchandise. She thought the idea very exciting and told her boss that she really knew her team would do a great job on the campaign.

But now Maria was definitely unhappy. She found herself trapped between her angry superiors, who thought she should be moving faster on launching global press releases, and her employees, who were continually arguing with Marketing around their plan for a big bash they were jointly responsible for in Madrid, now only six weeks away. She had a headache that just never seemed to end and a level of fatigue that bordered on exhaustion.

Getting up from her black granite-topped desk and walking to the floor-length windows that overlooked Lake Michigan, she thought of her reluctance to leave Chicago. She had been there now for more than fourteen years, and she knew well enough that anyone taking on new projects in the present economy could find themselves out of work at the whim of just one company executive who didn't think a particular project was moving fast enough. She hated feeling this vulnerable. She leaned up against the window with her arms crossed and almost locked in place. She closed her eyes. She could hear her heart beating as the room started to close in on her.

In the past during tough times she would ask herself a series of questions that would help her unplug from where she was to see possibilities opening up. Now, she asked, what had she learned since the last time she was really challenged in her job? Was she willing to slow down a bit to hear what her intuition was saying to her? Was she prepared, for example, to let some people go who were not ready for the changes their organization was going through? She had really grown to love her team, but not all of them fit with this new paradigm management was pushing.

The idea of her team readily partnering with Marketing without them creating collectively at least ten arguments a day seemed impossible. And if she did let people go, how could she find new hires who would get this new concept quickly? Most people were used to working autonomously or at least only with their own departments. Marie saw synergies between the two teams, but she also had difficulty convincing her team of these commonalities. She knew her other team partner in Marketing, Jackson Blake, felt the same thing happening with his communications between himself and his group.

Marie let out a deep sigh. It was actually taking longer than usual to get anything accomplished daily because of the tempers that were flaring between departments. She decided she would write down a few of the things she knew she could do today to help her change the direction her team seemed to be heading. She walked back over to her desk and still standing, opened up a Word document on her computer and started typing:

Set up a meeting with Jackson.

Call Darryl. Get insight as to how to proceed.

Take the afternoon off.

Darryl was the one person she knew could help her get off of dead center. She had counted on him before when she had to turnaround the office morale. He had been instrumental in guiding her through a process that helped her let go of her anger over what she saw as the right leadership for the project her team was working on, to a place of unguarded openness to doing things differently from what she would have chosen. Darryl definitely had a way of bringing people together from disparate backgrounds and helping them see how to leverage their diverse strengths.

He also had been her friend for more than ten years. They had been study partners at Northwestern where they had both gotten their MBA degree. Darryl had helped her go from a naïve new hire at Calcom Telecommunications to a manager and now to Director of Communications for the $1.8 billion company. Marie knew that Darryl would be honest with her – tell her what she might not want to hear, but needed to hear in order to accomplish her goals.

She just didn't know where he was because the last time she emailed him, she got a message back that he was on a sabbatical for a month. She wondered if some of their old friends might help her out. It seemed the people in his office were unwilling to divulge where he was, and without knowing the people he had been connected to in the last year, Marie was at a definite loss for finding him.

She decided to start with Jeremy Pastor. Jeremy had been in their study group. He might know where Darryl went, as they had gone on a few vacations together over the last few years. Jeremy, like Darryl, really enjoyed traveling to South America and Europe. She hoped that Darryl was someplace where he had access to phones. Sometimes the two of them would go off on extreme adventures into places where there were no satellites that supported phones. And Marie really wanted to talk to Darryl. She had a compelling feeling that time was of the essence as she dialed Jeremy's number in Houston.

"Hi Jeremy," Marie said with caution, hoping that she would find him happy to hear from her and hold some knowledge of Darryl's whereabouts. "It's Marie. How have you been?"

She waited while Jeremy paused, probably to figure out who Marie was. In the silence, Marie added, "Marie Ardent from B-school."

"Oh! Marie! Why this is a pleasant surprise!" She could certainly hear the Texan drawl coming out of Jeremy's mouth. Although Jeremy had been a native of Chicago, he had been in Texas for the past ten years, and obviously he had acquired more than success there. "What has you calling today? How have you been?"

"Oh, fine. I am sorry to bother you, Jeremy. I'm actually looking for Darryl. Have you seen him recently?"

"No, but I did just hear from him before he left for his sabbatical last week. Why? Is there something wrong?"

"Oh, no, nothing. It's just that I wanted to get in contact with him and I know he went on hiatus but I don't know where. We talk often, but somehow we didn't get a chance to speak before he left and he just emailed last week telling me about his time off. He forgot, however, to let me know where he might be going and he didn't leave a forwarding address. No one at his office seems to know where he went."

Jeremy laughed. "That's Darryl all right. I'm surprised he had time to send you an email."

Marie laughed too, but very lightly. She really needed to get in touch with Darryl, and although she was enjoying the conversation with Jeremy, she felt again an anxious push inside her to move the conversation forward. "So, did he say where he was going?"

Jeremy continued, "Yes, let me see… He said he had rented a chateau someplace in Europe. I know! He said he was going to someplace near Madrid!"

"Madrid?" Now her heart started beating faster.

"Yes, it just so happened that I had two tickets to the baseball game here in Dallas for the Rangers opening day. I was calling to invite Darryl since I hadn't talked to him in awhile and I figured it was a good reason for us to get together. But when I called his office at Dickson and McCabe, he sounded like he was in quite a hurry to leave. He said he was burned out and needed to get away before his employer gave him yet another new project to work on and so we cut our conversation short, and that's the last I heard of him. It's only been a week or so since he should have left, so I imagine he's still in Madrid."

Marie sighed again. Now she knew where he was, but how would she find him there? "Did he say where he might be staying in Madrid?"

Jeremy didn't say anything for a moment. She could hear him breathing into the phone and waited for him to answer. She remembered this was Jeremy's style. He always took time to ponder questions that he did not have a quick answer to and that he assumed people would just be patient in waiting for him to roam through the synapses in his neural network that resided in his brain. About a minute later she heard him say, "Wait, yes, yes there was someplace he said he was going. He said that he was going to rent a chateau somewhere around the countryside outside of Madrid. He also said that he was using the service on the Net that we used last summer when we went to Madrid and rented a place for two weeks."

With that statement made, Marie quickly finished the conversation with Jeremy, making sure she got the name of the service that they had used and quickly made calls to find out where Darryl was.

Three hours later Marie was on her way to the airport. She purchased a plane ticket to Madrid and made arrangements to rent a car to travel to Segovia, a quaint village about an hour or so outside of the city. She told her team that she would be communicating with them by email and that they were to continue on as they were, which wasn't good, but at least they were still talking. Right now, all she cared about was catching up with Darryl and brainstorming with him as to her next move. She had no time to waste. It seemed as if her job depended on it.

It seemed like hours (and it was) before she was finally on the ground at the airport in Madrid and then actually in a car to drive to Segovia. Everything seemed to go wrong from problems with the size of one of her carry-on bags to the car rental company losing her reservation. She had to wait two more hours for someone to turn in a car so that she had one she could use to drive to Segovia.

When she arrived in Segovia, it was just turning dusk. It was her favorite time of day. The beautiful midnight blue sky mixed with magenta and gold and appeared in sharp contrast to the huge aqueduct left over from Roman times. Segovia was nestled comfortably between two hills on the other side of the small mountain range that bordered Madrid to the north. In addition to the fabulous aqueduct, one of the most well-preserved relics from the ancient past in all of Spain, there arose atop one of the hills to the right of the town the brilliant silhouette of a fairytale castle.

Marie found herself almost gasping in astonishment at the town's beauty and the landscape. She was later to learn that this same castle in Segovia had made such an impression on a young Walt Disney many years earlier that he used an exact replica of it as the model for his classic film Sleeping Beauty, and later for his popular theme parks. She took a deep breath. The chill mountain air refreshed her like a glass of clear chardonnay. Despite her jet lag and near exhaustion, it was as if she had been transported back in time to a 10th century village in Europe. It was absolutely exquisite.

She drove slowly up to one of the several archways of the aquaduct and wound her car to the right, up the sharp incline of the bordering hill. She wove to the right and then to the left looking for a marker that would get her through the town and out beyond the castle where she knew Darryl was staying. When it seemed as if she was completely lost, she saw the road to the left, turned up it, and drove to the end where, she hoped (now somewhat desperately as it was getting darker) was Darryl's chateau.

She parked her car on an angle in a dusty gravel drive and went up to the door. For a moment she hesitated. What if he was here with someone else? She realized that she could very well be interrupting his social life and that he might not appreciate that. Yet, it was now too late.

She had come this far. At the very least, she could say hello and schedule some time in the next day or so when they could talk, that was if he had company. With that, she knocked upon the large oak door three times with all the strength her fist had at that moment.

※

*"Morality means to walk like others along the path."*
Chauang-Tzu, 3rd Cent. Philosopher

# CHAPTER 3
## The Meeting

Darryl opened the door, wondering who in the world had found him. He'd deliberately left obscure instructions to his executive assistant to ensure his privacy during this four-week hiatus. The only person he had spoken to right before he'd stumbled on the plane to Madrid, exhausted from his months of travelling and killer work schedule, had been an old friend from University who'd called just as he was leaving his home in Chicago. He turned the handle and opened the door.

"Darryl, I'm so glad I found you here!" Marie exclaimed as she threw her arms around Darryl, hugging her old friend.

Darryl took a surprised step backward. "Marie!" he exclaimed. He couldn't believe his eyes. His old studying partner from his university days was standing before him in Segovia, Spain. "How did you find me?"

"Jeremy told me where you were," she replied. "Of course he didn't know exactly where – but that's where my investigative skills proved themselves useful." She slipped out of his arms and looked imperviously around the chalet.

Darryl reached to help her take off her jacket. Simultaneously, Marie pulled at one sleeve to take it off. Their hands smacked into each other and they both laughed.

"Just like old times?" Darryl remarked. "We're still thinking almost too much alike that we run into each other's ideas, let alone bodies!" They both smiled at one another and Darryl continued, "I hope you haven't eaten, anticipating that I haven't either? I know it's way past dinner time in the States, but I wouldn't put it past you."

Marie shrugged her coat back on. "Oh, you know I haven't. And I know you well enough to remember you always 'go native' before you even get off the plane. You're a chameleon, adopting the culture and customs of any country you're in." She looked at him with that old smile of hers that he had forgotten, almost.

"Well," he replied. "Take a few minutes to relax and then we can walk down to the village and get something to eat. I'm dying to know what you are doing in Madrid and what you said to Jeremy to convince him to tell you where I was. I threatened him with severe bodily harm last week if he told anyone." He smiled at her to let her know that he wasn't unhappy with her arrival.

She replied simply, "Jeremy remembers what a good partnership you and I made in our study group and that we were better together than apart. When I told him why I wanted to get in touch with you, he knew that we'd both be better off by partnering than trying to figure this all out on our own."

Darryl looked thoughtful for a moment. "I always thought Jeremy was a sharp guy. Now I know it." With that, he picked up his own jacket, which he'd carelessly thrown over the back of the chair, and they left the chalet and walked down to the village in the warm Spanish night, the wonderful aroma of tapas flowing through the ancient streets luring them on.

✳

"Ah, Senior Mitchell. Welcome again." The Maitre de walked quickly around his reservation stand and reached out to shake Darryl's hand. Darryl smiled warmly at him and introduced Marie. "Manuel, good to see you. This is an old friend of mine from the States," he said, presenting Marie. "We went to university together in Chicago."

"Wonderful," replied Manuel as he took Marie's hand in his and kissed both her cheeks. He turned back towards Darryl and smiled again. "So I suppose you desire your favorite seating, senior?"

"Of course," said Darryl. He turned to follow Manuel as he led them through the crowded restaurant to a quiet table overlooking the garden.

"Senior," said Manuel, as they were being seated. "I wonder if you have had a chance to email my nephew, the one we discussed last week?"

"Yes, I have," replied Darryl. "I sent the full list of my business contacts in Chicago who are alumni from U of C, which you said was his first choice for Graduate School. One of my colleagues is a professor there and I think he'll be very helpful to Pablo. But certainly I plan on staying in touch with him and I'll make sure he's taken care of."

"Muchas Gracious! Thank you so much, senior, for your assistance." Manuel finished seating them and hurried away to solve a pseudo-crisis in the kitchen.

Marie eyed the restaurant and turned back to Darryl with a smile. "This is the first time I've been in Spain. I never realized that the people here were so friendly and open, or that they speak pretty good English, even this far away from Madrid."

Darryl quickly dispensed with the ordering of the wine and Marie allowed him to choose the meal. With that accomplished, he turned to her and said, "Now, tell me what's going on."

Marie looked down at her napkin and back up into his eyes. "Well, you know that I've been at Calcom Telecommunications for twelve years now, ever since we graduated, and I've never had a situation like the one I'm dealing with presently."

"And that is…?" Darryl didn't make it easy for her. He knew she needed a little pushing to get to the heart of what was troubling her so that it could be discussed and remedied. To his surprise, Marie, who was usually not so forthcoming, spoke very candidly.

"My team isn't partnering with Marketing very well. We need to quickly integrate our PR and marketing efforts or this new idea of ours in Madrid wont launch on time."

"Why?" Darryl asked.

"There seems to be a problem over who's really leading this initiative. Corporate tells us that we need to work together, but when it comes down to day-to-day decisions it doesn't seem to be happening. For example, the Marketing team wants us to host an event that will appeal to 20-30 year olds in our new Madrid market. Our research is showing that Spanish teenagers, the 13-19 year olds, are one of the largest emerging purchasers of mobile computing and cellular technologies...you know, phones, PDAs, whatever. We just can't seem to get aligned on this issue. Worst of all, my budget will only support one market rollout."

Darryl carefully sipped his wine and thought for a moment. There were some similarities between Marie's situation and his own.

"You know me," he replied. "I usually break my own problems into four components and then try to figure out which one is out of sync with the others. In consulting, it's pretty easy; there are people, process, technology, and strategy components to any problem. If something isn't working, it HAS to be one of those four that is misaligned. In your case, it sounds like a people issue."

Before Marie could respond they were interrupted by a loud 'Darryl!' coming from the center of the room. They both looked toward the voice and saw a tall well-dressed Spanish gentleman weaving his way through the maze of tables. Darryl rose from his chair in recognition and waited until the man arrived, extended his hand in greeting.

"Eduardo, how are you?" he asked.

"Excellente, my young friend," Eduardo replied. "And how are you and your lovely guest doing on this beautiful spring evening?"

Darryl replied, "Eduardo, I'd like to introduce my friend Marie, who is working in Madrid this week."

Eduardo approached Marie and carefully took her hand in his. "How do you do, Senorita?"

"Fine thank you," Marie said, smiling weakly. Darryl interrupted, seeing Marie's discomfort.

"Actually, we've been discussing something that you, as an educational trainer, might have a point of view on. It has to do with business, actually. Marie has an issue she is facing that requires rather immediate attention."

"Oh, really," responded Eduardo. "You know, we Spanish don't like to ruin a nice dinner by talking business. We prefer more interesting discussions on whether Real Madrid will win their next game or how to manage the waves of tourists flowing into our countryside in the next few months!" He laughed and looked at Marie and Darryl, and being an astute observer, noticed their faces, especially their eyes; both showed signs of disappointment, so he offered his help, looking at Darryl who had asked the question, "But if it is important to you, my friend, I will gladly help. In fact, my party is leaving now; we just came in for drinks and they have an important meeting in the morning. If you wish, I can remain with you and discuss whatever you wish."

"We'd really appreciate that," Darryl replied, holding out a chair for Eduardo. He took it and sat down at the table.

Darryl reached over and poured him a glass of wine. Eduardo sipped it and then turned toward Marie. "Tell me what I can do for you."

Again, Marie, who usually didn't open up so quickly, let alone to strangers, shared all the facts of her dilemma that she had just shared with Darryl, providing more details this time, such as her deep frustration over the lack of collaboration between her direct reports and the marketing department, as well as her fear over her own career and whether this problem might cost her her job. Darryl's obvious trust in Eduardo encouraged her to speak frankly.

Eduardo leaned back in his chair and placed his large hands on his knees. He looked thoughtful for a moment, and then spoke. "There is no question that you have a serious dilemma. But it is definitely something that can be solved. In fact, I know just what you should do."

Marie looked at him in astonishment and asked. "What?"

Eduardo replied, "Quit your job, move to lovely Spain, and spend your days tending to your vineyard and olive trees. That will solve all your problems." He looked at her seriously for a moment, and then burst out laughing. "I'm just kidding! You Americans are always so serious." His voice held a kindly note and he chuckled again.

Marie paused and started laughing with him. It felt good to have a release from the tension that she'd been feeling over the last couple of weeks. Darryl looked at the two of them as if they were crazy.

"No really, senorita. The real solution has to do with some people I know who have developed a process for building collaborative business environments."

Darryl and Marie simultaneously looked at him and both asked, "What does that mean?" They glanced at each other and each smothered a laugh at their synchronicity, again.

"They're called the Networlders," Eduardo explained. "The name comes from the awareness that decisions we make in a split second can affect our lives forever. And I know of a process that both speeds up your decision-making and improves it. Each split second can be used to expand a positive event or correct a negative one. The more conscious you are of your choices the more control you have over your situation and the more your life will become a meaningful extension of who you are and your values. It's about relationships first."

Darryl leaned forward across the table, tilting his head within inches of Eduardo. His eyes narrowed and he felt a quickening of his pulse.

Eduardo continued, "For example, Marie, in your situation you have people who are working to protect their own interests. It is very natural, therefore, that they would resist working with the other team, because as you've explained, they feel threatened by them. However, if they were offered the opportunity or the choice to have a conscious 'exchange' where they get to share their concerns, the conversation would more naturally revolve around things that would be of mutual interest and shared goals and not around areas of conflict or disagreement.

"The first step in a Networlding exchange is to identify the similar and complementary values that each person holds. What you'll probably find is that most of the members of both teams hold similar values such as trust, integrity, and cooperation. Once they reveal these values to each other, they will begin to connect in a new way. As the head of your department, you won't have to force people to work together; they'll naturally seek integration points with each other. In other words, they'll start having conversations that build off of shared values, and the walls of avoidance, frustration, and even downright anger will start to fall. Just getting people to listen to each other and share their values starts them on a path leading to better decisions."

Marie interrupted. "What I do know is that today trust is one of our top values because it's one that we always question the most. So what you're telling me is that if I can encourage, or rather if I can apply these concepts and enable my team to trust the marketing department, we'd all make better decisions?"

Eduardo replied. "It's the lack of directed conversation around this real issue of trust that is the first horn of your dilemma. The other horn is the 'contract' you make with yourself and your people to have these very personal conversations in the workplace."

Marie looked at Darryl and smiled. "How do these people manage to convince everyone that being this open really works?" she asked Eduardo.

"Well, there are four stages everyone goes through, as I think you know: Awareness, Recognition, Ownership, and Leverage. And you two are just at the Awareness stage yourselves. This is the first time you've even become aware that a real process exists that may help, even though you may be using some pieces of this instinctively in your daily work lives. After you become aware, you'll then recognize that this process can have some application in what you are struggling with. With recognition and some application, you'll take ownership of your own tailored way of Networlding with people around you. Once your colleagues and peers go through this process, the 'network effect' comes into play and you experience the ability to leverage the capabilities of you and your group, sharing your insights with others and actually developing new conversations that evolve your collective insights as to how to continuously work well together."

With that, Eduardo glanced quickly at his watch and grimaced. "Ah, I forgot. I have some items to attend to this evening. My apologies." He pushed his chair back from the table and stood up. Marie and Darryl rose as well.

"Thank you so much for the ideas," Marie said with a smile. She extended her hand to him, but he bypassed it and kissed her again on both cheeks. Darryl shook his hand and Eduardo departed. Before he had taken a few steps, however, he turned back with a smile.

"You know," he said. "I think there is a meeting coming up at the end of this week that you two might think about attending. It's one of the Paris chapters, or what we call circles of the Networlders, that will be getting together. I really think you might get a lot out of the discussion. Not to say the least that I think you both can add a lot as well."

Darryl looked at Marie and they both turned to Eduardo. "Of course we'll go," they both said simultaneously. Eduardo laughed and said that he'd email Darryl the location and time. With a dramatic wave of his hand, he departed, his large form weaving musically across the room until he was out of sight. Darryl turned back to Marie with a quizzical look on his face. "What do you think?"

"I think that if what he's saying about these Networlders is even half true, then I need to make sure I'm at that meeting."

"I agree," Darryl replied. "We haven't talked about why I'm here, but most of what he said may be a great help to me in my predicament as well." He looked at her with a quiet warmth.

"Isn't it odd that he was here tonight?" she asked. "I mean, what are the chances that we'd run into someone you've only met briefly and that he'd have such interesting ideas about problems that he can't possibly have faced as a trainer?"

"I wouldn't be so sure that he hasn't faced these types of problems," Darryl replied. "After all, he's responsible for delivering training to some of the largest companies in Spain, Telefonica, El Corte Ingles, GasNatural, and many others with hundreds of locations all over the country. Even though I just met him once, I know what he's accomplished here. There are many dialects and business customs in Spain. The variations in local cultures reflect themselves not just in different languages, but also in different ways of interacting with employees and customers. If Eduardo says that he's hooked up with an organization that 'gets it' and can help break through those barriers, then trust me, he has." Darryl looked up at the waiter as the food arrived at the table.

He smiled again at Marie and winked, "Let's enjoy the meal. Then you can tell me more about what you have been up to with your life in general since we last spoke. I know you were into kickboxing, canoeing and cycling; you'll probably tell me now that you have ventured into parachuting and extreme skiing!"

With that, the two of them chatted away for hours, sharing their individual adventures they had experienced over the last half year, letting the night embrace them with its warmth and sweetness. They stayed absorbed in their conversation until their waiter started to clean their table for the fourth time after dessert and they finally noticed that no other patrons were in the restaurant except them.

✳

*"Rules have no existence outside of the individual."*
Henri Matisse, French Painter, 1908

# CHAPTER 4
## The Circle

It was early afternoon of the following day.

Darryl had just returned from a long walk along the rich, always stimulating Spanish countryside. Meandering across the rock-strewn hillsides bordering the northern edges of Segovia, he'd been thinking about the conversations the night before.

The winds trawled off the mountains to the south with surprising vigour, as if seeking to hook fast and strip bare the modernity of the occasional satellite antennae or to push off into the unknown crevices the smattering of Volvos maneuvring through the turnabout below. The winds seemed bent on uncovering something, perhaps the ancient heritage of the small Castillas, the very foundations of both war-like and agrarian Spain, or the paved roads that wound like blackened tourniquets across the mountain side.

The cinnamon winds swirled mischievously across both the raw hillside bushes and his tousled hair. The air filled his lungs with the kind of sweet freshness he remembered from distant childhood springtimes in upper state New York. But here was a hint of wildness and spice that he'd never experienced in the States. The winds seemed to remember the Celts from the north, the Persians from the south, and the centuries of blood and family that made Spain such a magnificent, fascinating, mysterious country.

Darryl breathed deep a number of times. This was why he consistently came back to recharge his spirit. Spain was the home of an old, old civilization (some say the oldest), with a scorched middle ravaged by a thousand years of war and fire and yet existing with such independence, such defiance, such honor, that he couldn't help feel after a few weeks here that he too could set forth to the New World in the West and conquer them anew. This trip, the feeling was stronger than ever.

✳

Darryl sat at the antique writing desk in the corner of the living room and casually downloaded his email. The line speeds were so unbelievably slow, he was surprised he even stayed connected; but that was part of the enjoyment. ISDN was a foreign word in Spain. No use trying to receive a ten megabyte file from anyone – only text, and only when he wanted was his rule on holiday.

Surprisingly, when he looked at his inbox, a message from Eduardo concerning the Paris Networlder's meeting was already there. He sent a quick acknowledgment back and called Marie on her cell phone to let her know the exact date and time of the circle meeting. When she answered the call she sounded out of breath.

"Hi, Darryl," she answered quickly. "What's going on? I have someone on hold here and someone else from the States IM'ing me at the same time."

Darryl grimaced as he remembered all the times he had said that to callers who had phoned him at work. He was in week two of his hiatus and settled into a leisurely pace. Hearing Marie's frenetic voice brought back a rush of memories, not all of which he was proud of. Having a growing new perspective, armed with Eduardo's words, yet not far enough away from his own life that he couldn't feel for Marie's plight, he had a glimpse of an answer that might help them both.

"Marie, take a deep breath. Turn around and glance out the window. What do you see?" There was a moment's pause on the other end of the line. Marie had always trusted Darryl in the past and decided this time was no exception, even though this was the last thing she had time for today. So she swivelled her chair around and looked out the window behind her desk.

"I've turned and am looking out the window. I see the mountains to the north with some dark clouds hovering low over them," she said. "There's also some low lights coming from some of the outlying suburbs and some occasional traffic on the M30 I see in the distance."

"Ok, where would you rather be?"

Marie sighed on the other end of the line. "Ok, Darryl. I get it."

"Marie, you know I've been out of the daily grind for a enough days to have some perspective that could be of value. Why don't you tell me exactly what's going on right now?"

Marie took another breath. "Well, it's a typical Monday. It started right off the bat when I walked into the temporary office we've set up in Madrid. I was greeted with over a dozen emails from my team and Mark's team in the States. It seems that now the budget for this launch has been cut even more, and I can't see any way for us to get the talent necessary to be successful with the PR event, regardless of whose strategy is correct."

All of a sudden a brilliant idea flashed in Darryl's mind. He thought about his friend Blake from the UK; Blake had a younger brother who had steadily been climbing the Rock charts in London to the point where his last single had hit #10. He knew that if he asked, Blake could probably get his brother to cut his fees down to almost nothing to help out an old friend.

"I have a great idea. Listen to this." Darryl shared his idea with Marie, who immediately agreed to draw up a contract for Blake's brother if Darryl could arrange his support for the campaign within the next couple days. She had heard of him and knew enough about music to realize that he was an unusual cross-over artist who had captured both the teen and the thirty-somethings listening audience. If it worked and they could sign him for this special launch, it would definitely get her off the hook for having to deliver a launch campaign with nearly no budget. And, it would enable her to deliver a program that appealed to both target markets. Darryl's great idea would also help her out tremendously with the executives in her company, keeping them happy with her performance while allowing her an opportunity to prove her point in the marketplace.

"What other problems do you have today?" Darryl asked with a smile in his voice.

Marie laughed, realizing that her old friend had broken through her 'funk' and she now had a better handle on her day. "Nothing more important than that."

Darryl changed topics. "Good, then let me tell you about what happened today with regards to Eduardo. I received an email from him this afternoon and the meeting that he had talked about is actually at the end of this week in Paris. Are you up for a road trip?"

"If you can make it happen with this artist, I'll be able to take a couple days off this week, so yes!" she replied with renewed energy. They exchanged a few more pleasantries and then ended the call. They both were looking forward to continuing this adventure.

Darryl glanced out his window as he hung up the phone. From the corner of his eye he caught the silhouette of Segovia's fairy-tale castle in the distance. He suddenly felt a little like Don Quixote rushing to aid Dulcinea. But unlike the character in Cervantes' classic, he wasn't mad; he was more sound of mind than he had ever been. Like a knight equipped with a strong lance, he felt he had the ability to produce a result that would really make a difference for Marie's career. His hands working deftly across the keyboard, he charged forth and launched an email to Blake.

※

"Hello, my friends!" Eduardo smiled, throwing his arms around both Darryl and Marie and ushering them further into the private dining room at the rear of the restaurant. Marie looked around at the gorgeous wall hangings and grinned at Darryl. In the taxi ride down the Champs Elysses she had remarked at how the spring mist rising off the Paris streets made the town look like something out of one of the Matisse prints she had at home. Now she was getting a glimpse at the inside of a quaint old restaurant on Rue de Rivoli, at the edge of the shopping district (well, at least the edge of the tourist shopping district – there is no real edge to the shopping in Paris.). Across the street loomed the impressively lit Hotel de Louvre.

As Darryl and Marie entered the back room, they noticed a number of individuals clustered in a few groups with drinks in hand, conversing enthusiastically. Eduardo took care of ordering them an aperitif and started the introductions.

"Darryl and Marie, I want you to meet Hector, one of our circle leads in Madrid who is here helping the Paris circle get started." A swarthy Spanish-appearing man smiled widely at them and shook hands with them both. "Buenas Tardes, how are you?"

"And here is Pierre, Ana, Candice, and Sophie. They work for the same French company and have similar issues, I think, as you two have." The four greeted Darryl and Marie warmly in English, and then returned to a lightning-fast conversation in French amongst themselves.

"And here we have Gilles and Patrick. They don't work together, but have joined up to also help our fledgling Paris circle." The two smiled their greetings to Darryl and Marie. Eduardo continued to help them negotiate their way around the crowded room.

"And over here we have Guy from one of our London circles. He happened to be in town on business and, interestingly enough, used a Networld datalink to find out about this meeting and we welcome him as well." A young, fidgety Englishman, with a touch of the dandy in him, grinned at them both and offered his greetings.

"And finally, we have Higachi-san from Tokyo. Higachi-san is helping us expand our circles in Japan and was also over here on business, so we invited him to share some of his perspectives on communications and networking styles in Japan to see if they might help our circles in France."

Eduardo looked around the room and shrugged his

shoulders. "You know, it never ceases to amaze me, mi amigos, how quickly this concept is taking hold and providing value to our members. I remember just a few years back when the only activities were all in the States.

"We had some big questions as to whether it would even work outside the U.S., given the difference in cultures, languages, personal and business protocols, etc. Now, I'd dare say there are probably a hundred times more circles expanding every month outside of the U.S. than inside. That's thousands of people starting to link together based on common values! I can't imagine what this is going to look like a few years from now." He gazed at them expectantly.

Darryl took the cue. His gaze also swept across the room and returned to Eduardo's face. "I can't either, but I do know one thing," he said. "I've been Franklinized and Coveyized until I felt lobotomized. I've had Palm Pilots and Blackberrys. I've used email, voice mail and occasionally tried mental telepathy to communicate with my teams and my clients. I've investigated skills-based networking and behavior-based interviewing. I've reorganized dozens of global companies and started a few NewCo's as well. I've learned every 2x2 matrix for organizational enablement, communications, and change leadership ever created. At the end of the day, I haven't found a single thing that is universally replicable, reusable, or even relevant across individuals or industries in the same country, much less across countries or cultures.

"All I've found are communication principles so vague as to be un-implementable, and teamworking, shareworking, and networking practices so varied as to be unintelligible. Everything seems to come down to the quality of the person in charge. If they are good, then they can successfully implement bad models. If they are bad, then the best model in the world won't save them or the company. So I'm going to be very interested in the conversation tonight!"

Marie looked at them both and spoke up. "I don't have as much global experience as Darryl. I know he's practiced in Asia and South America as well as Europe and the States. But I do know one thing. There has got to be a better way to get things done. It just can't be this hard. I remember when I was in B-school, the military mantra we'd adopted for ourselves as the next generation of American business leaders went something like 'the difficult we do immediately, the impossible takes a bit longer'. Now, I'm not sure there are solutions to the impossible. And I think everything that's impossible in business is impossible because of the people involved. And," Marie paused for a brief breath before plunging on, "everything is a people problem at the end of the day. I know this sounds harsh, but I really think that people cause all problems. Whether we can solve them all, I'm interested in hearing about. But frankly, most problems get solved, unfortunately, by waiting for someone to die, retire, or get transferred!" She accepted her aperitif from the waiter, took a sip, and gazed up at them somewhat petulantly.

"Well," said Eduardo. "I see we have some skepticism here. That's good. That's healthy. Without skepticism, we cannot achieve total honesty with ourselves or our ideas. And lack of honesty leads to a lack of integrity. And without integrity, even Covey's quadrants become a meaningless exercise in deceiving ourselves."

He looked at them both and waved them to the table as the others were being seated. "Just keep an open mind and remember our conversation from the other night. I think you'll find this interesting."

✳

*"Between stimulus and response freewill chooses,*
*and that makes all the difference."*
Elie Wiesel, Night

# CHAPTER 5
## The Solution

Dinner was long cleared away.

The background hum of conversations outside the room and the occasional clatter of kitchen dishes had slowly dissipated over the hours. French dining being what it was, they had long since entered the early hours of the next day, yet all still sat in animated discussion around the table.

The tablecloth was littered with empty wine glasses, partially eaten pastries that Marie absolutely couldn't resist, and a number of expressos the group was nursing. Their discussion had continued unabated throughout the meal. Darryl and Marie had jumped in frequently, posing questions and asking for clarifying points of view. Now the group had settled into the kind of receptive mood that often occurs in small groups where everyone has had their say and listened to everyone else's say and now were ready to land on some common ground to reach closure.

Eduardo began the summation. "Estoy feliz. Esto no occure todos los dias!" Everyone laughed. Eduardo smiled in response. "What I'm trying to say is that I'm pleased with tonight's discussions. What we know about ourselves and our values is the first step to improving our relationships and opportunities for success. One of the more difficult things we've dealt with tonight is the American-centrism of Networlding. The fact that an idea emanates from America doesn't always mean that it has limited value in the rest of the world!"

"Yes," interrupted Higachi-san. "But the Americans don't really understand anything about the world except where the oil is…and it's not in Japan!"

Everyone laughed again, although Darryl and Marie just smiled. They realized it would take more than one meeting and frankly more than one lifetime for the inescapable image of America to change in the hearts and minds of the world's people. Perhaps the events of the last year were opening a small hole in the hearts of the world towards Americans, but there was a lot of real changes that needed to be made for the wealthiest and most powerful country in the world (and one of the youngest) to be greeted without some sarcasm, some skepticism, and a lot of wariness.

"What I mean to say," continued Higachi-san, "is that I also was very skeptical that this concept of 'values sharing' could be taken to Japan, and for one very simple reason: Work is work, not values. In Japan, we don't share values in the workplace. We respect people's privacy and personal life and expect them to respect ours. The work itself brings its own value, and for it to get done correctly, everyone needs to focus on company values, not their own individual ones. It is serious insult to ask about families or anything personal with a peer or subordinate. You'd never start a Networlding circle in Japan based on this American-only model of like-values."

"I agree," said Sophie, one of the founding members of the new Paris circle. "Candice and I have worked with our boss for over eight years; there's been late nights, long weekends, etc. And we couldn't tell you if he was married, much less if he had kids or was an accomplished pianist or anything. We French simply don't go there. Our work is our work, and our life is our life. Why should they mix?"

Candice nodded her head in agreement and said, "What you say is true, Sophie. I can think of a real example in France. Our 'cradle to grave' healthcare and education network, along with our culture of privacy, doesn't motivate people to develop personal or professional relationships outside of their normal spheres."

"Well," interjected Guy. "In London, it's quite a different story. We thrive on 'The Scoop.'" He smiled at them. "I can't imagine someone new being in the office more than a day before having someone, a secretary or whomever, come up and introduce themselves and talk about their kids, their garden, the pain they get sometimes from the mole behind their left ear... everything goes!"

"Yes, and look at your illiteracy rate and your tabloids," retorted Candice. "No thank you."

"Now, now," added Eduardo. "Let's stay on the topic." He turned to Higachi-san. "If you had all these doubts, why did you try a few years back to start the first circle in Japan, and why do you think it has successfully replicated itself a dozen-fold now?"

Higachi-san took a sip of his still steaming tea. "Because of one simple fact. Communities exist. Values exist. You Europeans," he turned to face the French and Spanish contingent, "you think Americans watch television, eat at McDonalds, and adopt all the same values. Anyway, when a method or a model arises from America, you greet it with skepticism, as did I, because you are individualistic. You French, for example, don't feel there are communities in France the same way there are in the United States. You certainly don't feel that your people join together very easily with common sets of beliefs or behaviors. The failure of community-based eBusinesses in France attests to this. But I disagree.

"The very fact that there has been such a long-term universal disdain for the American business model, but grudging respect for the Americans who work here, is in itself a value! Everywhere I go in France I hear the same 'ignorant American' stories in business. You seem to have rallied around a common set of values: disdain for Americans!" He smiled at them and added. "My experience in Japan in shepherding the Networld model there also suggests the contrary. In Japan, we have different issues to overcome, mainly our reluctance to bring known values or opinions into the workplace. You have the issue of individualism and anti-Americanism to battle here. We have the issues of a stricter adherence to the social and business hierarchy and a stricter sense of our place in the company and the community, which limits dramatically this Networlding idea of free-forming, organic values-based networks of like-minded people."

"Wait," interjected Darryl. "I think we've heard these arguments tonight in a number of forms. I'm as curious as Eduardo as to your point of view on exactly why this model has started to work in Japan. What have you seen or done to do this?"

"Kieritsu," replied Higachi-san.

"Huh," responded Darryl, knowing the word, but not understanding.

"It's Kieritsu, but the real model, not the skeleton that you westerners took and adopted to serve your needs in the '90s. I sat and thought long and hard after I came back from my first Networlding meeting in Chicago a few years ago. And the more I thought, the more I realized that Japan's eleven-year recession and many of our economic problems were at the heart more of a people problem than anything else.

"That's when I went back and reminded myself of the original Kieritsu models and how they worked. Here, let me show you." Higachi-san got up and went to the flipchart at the front of the room, which had stood untouched throughout the evening. He swiftly drew a picture.

"Now this may look like a circuit board diagram," he continued from the front of the room. "But this is the reality of Japanese networks in business. And I knew right away that I couldn't 'beat' a system of interacting that had evolved over a few thousand years, so I had to find a way to leverage it."

Darryl and Marie looked at each other at the same time. They both smiled. Synchronicity again. This time, they knew the other was thinking that Higachi-san had just hit the nail on the proverbial head. Instead of trying to change the worlds they lived in, they both had to find ways to leverage them. They turned their attention back to what Higachi-san was saying.

"So, the dark lines represent the formal segregation of authority within our businesses, but also represent the formal lines of communication and interaction that we all have at work and in our communities. But notice that all the nodes (people) in this model have lines criss-crossing across formal lines! That's reality. People talk, even in Japan." And he looked again at Sophie. "And even in France.

"Never underestimate the power of our informal networks. Virtually all actionable knowledge is transferred; and therefore many decisions are made and much change occurs via the influence of the informal networks that exist. This isn't a problem to fix; it's an opportunity to leverage. That was my secret entrance to the castle. Behind all the structure and formality was a thriving pattern of body gestures, looks, emails (rarely), and other connection points in which like-minded people were communicating with each other. In the office, in the streets, in the karaoke bars, it was all the same. Behind the formal face of Japanese business was the human reality of people wanting to connect, wanting to reach out and learn from others like themselves, and doing it, albeit in a haphazard way. And that was all it took." He replaced the marker and walked back to take his seat. He took a careful sip of his tea and looked about the room.

"What do you mean that was all it took!" exploded Marie. "So what happened? How did you get your group together? What does all this have to do with the Kieritsu business model?" She looked with exasperation at first Darryl and then Eduardo. Higachi-san sat impassively.

Darryl spoke. "I think I can guess. Higachi-san realized quickly that if the model was perceived to be American-originated, or even if he took carte blanche the American ways of organizing it, then he was doomed. The secret of the original Kieritsu models, and the ones still in existence in Japan today, is the idea of 'synthesis' not 'compromise'. This means that when two companies find themselves doing business together, they have two choices to how they want to work together. They can decide to negotiate terms of purchasing, shipping, collaborating, or whatever involves each side having to give up on some points, as in a compromise.

"Or they can avoid these 'transaction-oriented' negotiations and look at the ways in which each company can enhance the total value of their combined operations. This is a much different discussion and results in what I'd call synthesize, not compromise. A synthesized result is not both sides giving up something, but both sides getting something. This was the promise of the early eBusiness models in the USA, but we weren't fully truthful about the gives and takes with each other, nor did we really integrate our operations and develop a mutually beneficial market model, like the Japanese had done long ago. Once Higachi-san found the Japanese way to implement the idea, I imagine it was easy from there." He looked over at Higachi-san. "Am I right?"

"Of course you are," Higachi-san replied. He then turned to Marie and added, "My first circle met in a Karaoke bar and I sang "The Girl From Ipenema" to open the meeting." Darryl's stifled laugh interrupted him; he absolutely loved that song.

Higachi-san continued. "Certainly no one there thought the meeting was anything more than a casual get-together. I was in charge of selecting the first attendees. I know that's not the American model where participants self-select their circle partners. In my case, most of the initial participants I selected were secretaries from my office. I found they had many things in common regarding their work challenges and opportunities so I couldn't resist sharing the Networlding process. Needless to say, it all worked out great, and the last new circle I shepherded into existence was for the chief marketing officers of ten of the largest banks and utilities in Japan."

Eduardo stood up. "I want you all to know that I asked Darryl and Marie to attend tonight not because they are part of one of our circles, but because they are facing, like all of us, many difficulties in their working lives." He went on to summarize both their situations with amazing accuracy. Darryl glanced at Marie and they both shook their heads slowly. Eduardo was quite perceptive behind his mannerisms. Eduardo turned to them and said, "I think you are getting a sense of what is involved in applying these concepts to specific problem situations. Before we get into it, I want to ask Ana," and he turned to her expectantly, "to give us an update on Paris Circle activities so far." He sat back down and Ana stood.

"I am pleased to do so, Eduardo," she said with a lilting quality to her voice and a soft French accent. She turned to Higachi-san. "What you've said is amazingly similar to what Sophie, Patrick, Gilles, and the rest of us have concluded about our own Paris circle. Overcoming our own biases just made us that much more concerned over being able to overcome other's biases in the business community here about this kind of 'forced' networking model." She looked about the room with the famous impervious French disposition, and succinctly continued.

"Honestly, we're so busy working, we often don't take time to focus on certain things that can help us acquire new critical and collaborative skills. To this point, when I was 'coerced' or perhaps the proper English word is 'coaxed' into attending a meeting of Networlders, I started to realize the value of focusing on these small changes that can make big differences.

"I also realized that many of my business experiences could have been a lot different if I had thought through a more conscious way of building and maintaining my professional relationships. I was always good at making initial connections and finding common values with my boss and the department heads I was working with. The thing I realized is that after all these years, I didn't maintain my network well enough. For example, during assignments I was able to get work done faster and more easily and the final product was indeed better. However, each time I started a new assignment, I didn't maintain my previous relationships.

"Except for the occasional business dinner, I really never expanded my network at all or connected what I've come to know as my Networlding circles across assignments. The very thing that I thought was wrong with Networlding, mainly that it was 'purposeful' and 'directed' collaboration, is what makes it so effective and rewarding. And so we," and she waved her hand to include her fellow French constituency, "have determined to grow our relationships by co-creating opportunities whenever we have the chance, and over time re-create our networks to realize even more opportunities. My suggestion for you, Marie, is not to reach out and try to find common values between yourself and the marketing department. My advice to you is to reach in and find those set of common values yourself.

"With a better understanding of your own values and how to share them with others, you'll find it easier to create situations where those values will shine through. I guarantee you'll immediately know when the connections are being made and when a value-exchange begins."

"Thanks," Marie replied, looking thoughtful. "And you know, I would have guessed that you were going to give me some story about reaching out and trying to connect with Mark and his team on a different level. And I would have told you to go pound sand!" She smiled at Ana, who smiled back. "But what you're really saying is quite unique. Instead of an outward-in method of finding common ground, I need to take an inward-out approach. I never would have thought that would be a process that would work in America." She laughed. Ana laughed too, and continued.

"You heard what Higachi-san said. He had to look inside first to find that approach from the inside of Japanese culture that would work with these concepts. The same is true in every country and with every individual. We all have to know where we start from to know how to get where we are going."

Marie looked at Darryl and smiled. She was beginning to get an idea that could give her more than a successful new product launch in Madrid. Now Hector spoke up.

"And Darryl, if what Eduardo says is true. You should have a very easy time making the transition from your current networking approach to this idea of Networlding." He looked at them carefully and then continued, "Believe it or not, I was born in Texas, am of Mexican descent, and have lived the last half of my life in Spain…mainly because I like the weather." He smiled mischievously at them. "I know what it is like to try to adapt my language, my style, and my ideas to the local culture and to my clients. I believe that you are already wired into your clients' past and present. The nature of business is both to pursue the opportunities at hand and to never let a relationship die, right? The problem is that many business people – consultants, salespeople, business executives forming alliances, etc. – usually focus on opportunities first, only building strong relationships on the back end. In contrast, the Networlding process focuses first on building key strategic relationships and then co-creating opportunities in a partnership dynamic.

"You don't have the same problem that Ana has by letting her business contacts grow stale, or what Marie has in trying to be successful in a corporate environment with bureaucracy and conflicting objectives. You simply have to take your haphazard network and turn it into a focused, cohesive Networld."

Darryl interrupted. "Wait a minute. I don't think you really understand. Often in consulting, I don't have the opportunity to start with a strategic relationship first. For example, I may be given an assignment worth $20M from a CEO who really dislikes me, but he knows I'm the best choice to get the job done, or I may be asked to do crisis-work for a client 10,000 miles away. So in essence, my network is frequently forced upon me based on the exigencies of the global market. Not my choice." He sat back, crossing his arms in front of him and frowned.

"No, no!" exclaimed Hector. "You don't understand. I know that often you have your network forced upon you, and that many of your business relationships don't necessarily fit your values. What we are saying is that you have a choice as to what your future relationships will be. You could begin building strategic relationships if you start by forming a Networlding infrastructure that will enable you to collaborate on key opportunities; that's why we created the circles. I can't imagine why you wouldn't be free to pursue any future career to your heart's content, or take the concept of these Networlding circles back to your current company and perhaps even change the world in doing so."

Darryl looked thoughtful and did not respond. Eduardo looked about the room and clapped his hands on the table. "That's enough for tonight." He turned to Darryl and Marie. "I only have one more thing to add." Groans rose from across the table and he whirled about. "No, I promise. Just one more brief thing."

"You don't know what the word 'brief' means, Eduardo," said Guy from the end of the table, with a smile.

"Ah, my friends, my enemies! Alas that I should see the day when my closest confidants shall turn on me like dogs!" He smiled and turned back to Darryl and Marie.

"I leave you with one final comment. And that is you must always think about 'touch-points'. Touch-points are those situations where your life and someone else's come together. They can be as brief as crossing each other's path on the sidewalks of Manhattan, or they can be as long as a lifetime relationship. Let me tell you a story to illustrate my point." Eduardo ignored the soft groans that came from across the table.

"When I was a boy going to school in Salamanca, we had a very old school building that had to be constantly cleaned or else creatures, insects and the like, would arrive in such numbers as to make studying nearly impossible and the building nearly uninhabitable. Each morning as I arrived in the classroom, I saw the gentleman who cleaned the school exiting as I was entering. He had the worn hands of a man whose life had been spent doing manual tasks. Yet he had a smile and a spring to his step that caught my eye as I arrived at school each day. That year, I had a science teacher who was most extraordinary. We had been studying all year for our final exam and on the day of the test, I felt I was very prepared. I had sharpened my pencils, arranged my notes, and stiffened my resolve to, as you say in America, 'ace' the test. We didn't have laptops in those days to help!

"Upon working on the exam for a few hours, I arrived at the final question, which was worth 40% of the test score. It was a simple sentence. 'What is the name of the janitor?' I was shocked. What kind of question is that on a final science exam?

I rose from my seat and approached my teacher to ask the very same question. He just smiled and waved me back to my chair. After puzzling for nearly one half an hour, I finally realized that I did not know the janitor's name and I couldn't possibly recollect ever even speaking to him during the year. I did the only thing I could do. I guessed." Eduardo looked at them sheepishly.

"And I guessed wrong, of course. The next week when we were all protesting our scores, the teacher raised his hand to silence the class and said something I'll never forget. He said 'Scientists observe. They don't select the facts to examine; they examine them all. They don't filter the facts to favor a theory; they face them all. And that man who cleaned this room every day of this school year is as much a factor in your learning as anything I've done up here at this desk. That's knowing your facts. And now you won't forget it.'" Eduardo looked at the two of them.

"I never have forgotten it. It's been the foundation of everything I've done in corporate training and development work. After the school year ended, I found out where the man lived and visited his house many times. I found out what a wonderful family he had, with grown sons apparently quite successful, and we became good friends over the years I was growing up.

"Many years later, when I was finishing my graduate work and was home for the weekend visiting my family, I stopped by his house. He greeted me as warmly as he had the first time, when I was a shy young kid perring over his gate. Over cerveza on his front porch, I told him that I was graduating soon and looking for work in the city. He looked at me quietly and went back into the house. I thought for a moment that I had offended him with my offhand remarks of my future work. But he returned a brief time later and handed me a business card. He said to me, 'This is my son. He works in Madrid. Look him up when you are done with your studies, and I'm sure he can help you.'

"I accepted the card without looking at it, almost embarrassed that this blue-collar man would make me such an offer. I really cared for the old man and didn't want to appear as if I was looking down on him when he had just shown me such a wonderful gesture of friendship. We finished our beers, and I warmly departed. As I was walking back up the road, I took the card from my pocket and looked at it more closely. I stopped dead in my tracks. Do you know what it said?" He looked around the room, but there were no groans now and no volunteers with an answer.

"It said 'Jose Gonzalez Alonzo, President, Telefonica'. His son was the president of one of the largest companies in the world. And two weeks later, when I met Jose, he offered me my first job out of school and has been a tremendous influence on my life ever since." Eduardo sighed deeply and said. "From that day in class and throughout all my visits to his father's house, I have been a human scientist. I observe myself. I observe others. I seek to find common ground. The sparks that come from these touch-points, the synchronicity that exists between people of like values and aspirations, the viral nature of relationships and the chain-reactions that occur between people when there is a purposeful effort to cultivate and grow their own 'Networlds', my friends, it is something to honor and understand."

With that, the rest of the group rose from the table and amid much pleasantries, said goodbye to Darryl and Marie and made their way out into the Paris night. Darryl and Marie walked outside with Eduardo and waited for a taxi. When it arrived, they both got in and waved goodbye. Darryl sat back in his seat and looked at Marie. She looked back. They both knew this was going to change their lives.

✳

*"Show me a hero and I will write you a tragedy."*
F. Scott Fitzgerald, 1936

# CHAPTER 6
## The Giver

It was week-three of Darryl's hiatus when he found himself driving from Segovia back to Madrid. The winding road leading to the metropolis was a fantastic diversion, ascending up past the snow-line and then descending down into hairpin turns all the way into the flatlands where far ahead lay the youthful and ageless town of Madrid.

The previous day when Darryl was casually checking email he'd noticed a message from many days before that he had overlooked. It was from one of his friends, Dawn, whom he had forgotten was living temporarily in Madrid. Actually, he hadn't really forgotten her rather insistent email message. He'd simply wanted to stay far away from any contact with people who knew him, preferring the anonymity of the Spanish countryside to the camaraderie of an American friend abroad.

He'd once travelled from Chicago to Dusseldorf, to Paris to Buenas Aires, to Santiago to Pucon, Chile in the course of 72 hours for the very purpose of getting as far away from marble floors, double-sealed corporate glass, and antiseptic conference rooms as he could. But this time, when he read the email, he paused to reflect. The meeting last week in Paris had made an impact, and he was curious about the new channel of thinking that was beginning to preoccupy him.

The woman who had emailed him, from the tone of her message, appeared to be facing the same challenges of 'storming the castle' in the workplace. As Darryl was driving into Madrid that afternoon to meet her for dinner, he was thinking hard. Relaxing music hummed in the background of the 2000 Volvo Convertible he'd rented upon first arriving in Madrid. The countryside was a landscape of rich greenery framing a blue sky delicately streaked with a brush of scarlet from a sun setting on a day washed clear by the rain the evening before. His racing thoughts moved in concert to the speed of his car. At the same time as he was driving and reflecting, his friend was experiencing quite a different, and more difficult, atmosphere at work.

※

"Que tal," Dawn said as she entered her boss's office in Madrid.

"Not bad," he replied. "But I have a problem with the latest reports you've given me." He glanced up at her as though expecting an immediate reaction. She remained impassive until she saw him tapping his foot, something he only did when he was about ready to launch into a tirade.

"What is it?" she asked. Her voice took on a cautious tone. She glanced out the office window as he paused to answer. Plaza Torre Picasso was the largest building in Madrid, in Centro Commercial en Castallana. They were on the 34th floor with a magnificent view of the setting sun over the plains to the west. The scarlet sky presented a soothing counterpoint to the tension in the room.

"Dawn, I can only conclude that either you are incapable of performing this job or unwilling to. This analysis you gave me is what I would expect from an intern or grad student – not one of our highest paid American analysts!" He looked up from his paper-filled desk with a sharp glance at the young woman standing before him.

Dawn stared in return, sighing to herself on the inside. She'd half expected it. After all, it had been six months since she had taken this overseas assignment and her expectations of a softer culture, a more casual approach to business in Europe than she had experienced in eleven years in the Manhattan meat-grinder, had been dashed early in this assignment, especially after she started working directly with Francois, the French strategy executive sitting before her.

American brashness and arrogance had extended even here – to the 50's style offices of the largest utilities company in Spain. She sighed again. Her workaholic lifestyle had nearly killed her in the States. Unable to really bring balance to her life, she'd had enough moxie and self-awareness to force a transfer oversees as the only way she might be able to find something more than dates with shallow executives, workouts at the club, and weekends on the internet.

All her life she'd given everything she had to her job. She loved it. Her intelligence and energy won her immediate friends among peers and relationships among senior executives. Not that it was her heart's desire, but the glass ceiling seemed thin and breakable in her early years at McKracken and Owen, one of the hottest market analysis firms in New York. But somewhere along the road she'd begun to encounter resistance, and it puzzled her greatly. It took all her skills to realize finally that people were rejecting her assistance...and that the resistance she felt was coming from herself as she slowly recognized this and reacted to it. She knew then that she was dissatisfied with the tradeoffs she'd been forced to make to achieve her goals and with the barren corporate culture she'd grown more and more numb to. In a mortified rush, she'd transferred to Europe to recover her priorities and reinvigorate her life.

She turned to face the balding, embittered countenance of her local boss, Francois, himself recently transferred to Madrid from Paris. "I'd say that you haven't read it carefully enough," she replied cautiously. "The local market for those services is 2-3 years behind what your marketing department has projected. The data is clear. If you proceed in rolling out the full campaign, your only hope is that the board doesn't read this report and realize you could have adjusted the timeline and saved the company hundreds of millions of Euros." She looked at him squarely; her American posture held out like a baton – waiting for him to strike or seize. He scowled over his glasses at her and waved at his paper-strewn desk.

"This is the result of your analysis!" He raised his voice one level. "Everyone in my department is now wasting valuable time rebutting your position before the board meets tomorrow when they should be finalizing the campaign and getting our messages out into the market!

"Now I want you to seriously consider what you are going to say in front of the board tomorrow morning. And I want you to remember just exactly why we brought you over here and how woefully short of our goals your achievements have been." He glanced at her one more time and sharply returned his attention to the papers scattered on the desk in front of him.

She looked curiously at him a moment longer then quickly left the room. Taking bare minutes to pack her laptop and reports for the next morning, she left the building and walked briskly down Paseo de Castallana, still seething in the warm Spanish evening.

Everything about this new job was beginning to irritate her. She didn't get it. Instead of escaping her problems and beginning anew, she had taken them with her. She wasn't quite sure how she was responsible for the current situation, but it felt similar to conflicts she'd had in Manhattan. Why were people not recognizing her contributions?

Although she wasn't an expert in the local market or the proposed service enhancements that the company was planning, she did know how to dissect market facts and how to tell the difference between data and information, between market noise and market indicators. Everything in her experience shouted that this strategic move the company was making wasn't ill-designed, just ill-timed. Why wasn't she able to communicate that effectively?

The utility markets in Western Europe were deregulating by 2003, but the consumer base simply wasn't ready for the kind of sophisticated single-point-of-contact relationship with their utility company that the marketing department and the head of strategy were proposing. It hadn't worked in the UK a few years earlier, and it wouldn't work here in Spain in the beginning of the 21st century. Their sales estimates were as aggressive as many of the dot.com business plans she'd reviewed back in the bubble economy of the mid '90s in the States…and just as unattainable.

She sighed and turned the corner onto the side street where her corporate flat was located. There was a small shop near her home. She waltzed into the tiny, family-run store and bent down quickly to sweep up an assortment of fresh fruit as a dessert to complement the tapas she had prepared yesterday for tonight's dinner. She'd finally received a response to an email she had sent an old friend who was visiting from the States. She'd immediately invited him over for dinner to get another opinion on her situation, and he'd accepted. A meal of homemade tapas, a nice bottle of Faustino Uno, and fruit compost for dessert was just the thing to end her day on a better note, and maybe get her moving on a track to solve her problem once and for all. However, she was worried about the board meeting in the morning.

✳

"That was wonderful," Darryl said as he finished the last of the fruit and wiped his mouth with the tan and blue cloth napkin. The dining room table was littered with empty plates and a three-quarter empty bottle of good Ribera del Duero. He pushed back his chair and glanced over at his old friend.

"Dawn, why don't you tell me what's bothering you?"

Dawn looked up from the last of her dessert and glanced quickly down again. "I didn't think it showed so much."

"Listen, Dawn. I've known you for years. We had dinner six months ago at the Manhattan Ocean Club and you told me you were coming here to get your life straightened out. I didn't say so at the time, but I was wondering what it was that needed straightening. One thing I did know, which you obviously didn't, is that your problem wasn't M&O or Manhattan. Your problem was you."

"Now wait a minute," Dawn interrupted. "That's not fair. You know as well as I do that unless you're a killer in a suit you can't succeed in Manhattan. And even then, being successful and staying successful are two different things. Eventually you move up or you burn out. I left before the latter happened to me."

"Are you sure?" he asked softly. Dawn looked at him closely and then looked away.

"Listen," he continued. "I know you pretty well. You came here to straighten out some priorities; that's fine. But how do you straighten something out? You grab both ends and pull tight. That approach assumes three things. First that you know where the 'ends' are. Second, that you have the ability to grab 'em and hang on. And third that you're strong enough to pull tight and keep pulling tight. What I see tonight is someone who may still be looking for one of the ends. So what's up?" He took a final sip from his wine and leaned back in the chair.

Dawn looked up at him again and sighed. "You're right. I am stuck. Creative block. Communications block. Intelligence block. I don't know. All I know is that I reached the end of the line at M&O in the States and had to get out. Had to escape. Anywhere. I even thought of taking that teaching position I'd been offered a while back."

She took a final sip of her wine and leaned back in her chair. The bright night of Madrid's downtown shone through the open double-windows at the far end of the dining room. The distant sound of the year-round revelers drifted through the windows. She continued.

"'I'm mad as hell and I'm not going to take it anymore' if you remember that saying. It's not fair. I feel like I'm just getting used all the time. Work used to be fun; now all I do is deal with people who get angry when I try to help them. And I really do want to help. In fact, that's been my intent all along in business – to really help others. I care about making a difference. That's where my passion lies; yet, it seems with every project I work on lately I run into big male egos and ugly office politics. I can't win." She looked down at her napkin, her face flushed with frustration.

He replied quickly. "Don't hide behind the male ego story or office politics. There's always more to it and you know it." He got up from the table and began to gather the plates for the kitchen.

"What do you mean?" she gasped?

"I think you might be giving too much and it bothers people." Darryl replied matter-of-factly.

"What are you talking about; I give too much? Isn't that what every company wants – employees who will dedicate themselves to their jobs like I do?"

"That's exactly my point," he replied. "You give so much, sharing your objectives and the facts that you uncover through your analysis of the financials or the markets or whatever, but you pay little attention to how you're interacting with people." He deposited the plates into the sink and picked up a towel to wipe off the table.

"You give and you give and you give. You take everything you have, your intellect, your energy, your passion for perfection and doing the right thing, and you lay it on the line every time you write a report or review a business plan or make a presentation. Don't you see?" he asked.

Dawn just sat there at the table, staring at the wall in deep thought, so Darryl continued. "It's too much. People think you have a hidden agenda. They didn't believe there was a purist in the heart of Manhattan, and they don't believe there's one here in the heart of Spain. There are things you want out of the work you do with others but you don't ask what their expectations are and you don't tell them what yours are, and then you get frustrated when they aren't pleased with your efforts. You passively pursue perfection and ask for nothing visible in return. And that bothers people."

Darryl sat back at the table and poured a couple of espressos for Dawn and himself from the small carafe.

He paused a moment until Dawn finally looked at him, this time with a sad, pained expression on her face. He said softly, "Dawn, let me tell you something that I've only just realized.

And by no means am I an expert or have it fully worked out myself. I figure there are basically three ways people go through life, whether it's business or your personal life. They give, they take, or they exchange.

"Now, most people only really practice the first two forms of connecting with others, but it's really the third from of connecting – exchanging – that really changes your life for the better. People who only take are the selfish slugs you worked with every day in New York and maybe here again in Madrid. They're in it for themselves and usually don't care if it's noticeable or not. They use people to achieve their goals and then they move on. It's the stereotype of American business philosophy – kill or be killed. Win or lose. And the smarter you are or more power you have or more networks you establish, the easier it is to fall prey to the temptation to 'take' and give nothing in return.

"On the other hand, people who give, like you, can be just as bad. They don't interact with the world, in business, or personal situations with any sense of how they impact those around them. In other words, they create a vacuum of guilt or remorse or just envy in others or they may eventually resent their giving later. The perception they leave is one of output with little or no input. It's a balm for the ills of the business, or for the customers, or for the accountants, or whomever. On the personal side, it's a balm for the ills of the relationship, supporting without asking for support and helping without asking for help. Givers don't seem to need anything for themselves. We may wear suits and fly across the world, but inside we still deal with stress and conflict the same way. It's fight or flight. When people have to deal with unusual situations, they either fight or get out. So if you're giving without requesting anything in return, that's a conflict for most people with whom you are connecting.

"They can perceive you as malicious with ulterior motives or naïve. Either way, in personal relationships, it may cause them to leave. Whereas in business relationships, they may choose to fight rather than leave, particularly if they have position power over you."

"I disagree." Dawn replied. "I know that neither I nor anyone else really gives needing nothing in return. Maybe asking nothing in return – but needing – sure, I'll concede that. For example, everyone needs balance. That's the one reason I escaped New York and came here. I came to realize that it's impossible to live my life and rely on work to feed me. What is possible, I thought, is to choose the 'currency' that I am to be compensated in. When people give money to charity or time to the peace corp or help to the church, for example, they accept payment in the currency of satisfaction, good feelings, or just knowledge that they are making a difference."

"Wait, wait," Darryl interjected. "My point is that as a giver, on the outside, you seem too good to be true. That's why people react badly toward you. They think you are hiding something."

"Well," interrupted Dawn. "For most givers, if I am one, the 'currency' I choose to be paid in may not be visible to those around me. For instance, personally, I can be in a relationship with a person I love, but who isn't supporting me and yet I can still be okay with it because I'm being fed with the satisfaction of knowing I'm making that person's life better.

"Similarly, in business, I can stay at a company a long time and not get promoted, but be okay with that because I'm being fed knowing that I'm making a difference, or that I love my work and it's the right place for me to be."

Darryl paused to take another drink of his coffee. He slowly put his cup down before he responded. "But the other option, the option to exchange, would provide you with both the giving that you love doing and the opportunity to create more dynamic and growing relationships. Exchanging involves thinking about the expectations you have in your relationships with others and letting others know what you would like to receive from them.

"This applies to both personal and business relationships. Exchanging in a business environment, for example, might look like you sharing with others what you can offer. In other words, the value you bring to the relationship. Here, you might exchange the great marketing skills you have for support in getting your project done on time. It's best to share these expectations verbally and often in writing, so that all parties know what is expected of them—what each party brings to the table for a successful exchange. Here, it is clear that you have created a mutually-beneficial relationship."

Dawn looked at him. "Darryl, I think you have interesting ideas, but I'm not sure I believe all this about givers, takers, and exchangers. I think you have too simplistic a model to describe things. The complexities of what we go through in life just can't be summarized in three words. It's never that simple. It's always some money thing, or political thing, or whatever thing that influences people. Sometimes I give asking nothing in return in personal relationships and they've ended on the rocks. Other times I've not given enough and I've lost wonderful people.

"At work, sometimes I've bailed out on a tough project because I didn't like the executive involved, or the value proposition, or the politics. In retrospect, some of those situations worked out fine and some didn't. But how am I supposed to know when to bet everything on an idea or a person, and when to hold back and work the 'model' as best I can? I think I need to think about this a bit more."

Darryl got up from the table. "Of course. I understand. And realize, I'm not an expert here. I just got back from a meeting in Paris that is starting to change the way I think about these things. Or rather," and he paused for a moment, "rather, I think it confirmed some of the things I've believed in and have been trying to do for a long time. Someday soon I'll share more about it and how I'm thinking about some interesting changes in my own career."

He walked over to the couch and picked up his jacket. "I've got to head back first thing in the morning, so I need to get back to my hotel. You take care of yourself, ok?" He looked closely at her.

Dawn rose from the table and joined him at the door. "Of course I will. I won't let those guys get the best of me! And I promise I'll think about what you said." She smiled at him.

He smiled back. "Hey, I have an idea. There's another meeting I'm going to in a couple weeks of a group of people who call themselves 'Networlders.' I've hooked up with this group because they have similar ideas about building mutually beneficial relationships. Why don't you come?"

Dawn looked a little dubious. "Where is it?"

"Well, I know they have a learning center, or corporate retreat location, outside of Madrid and another in Napa Valley, as well as community centers in a number of cities in the States and abroad. But I think this meeting is in Italy, where the Vienna circle gets together frequently." Darryl replied. "I'll email you the logistics. I think you'd really enjoy it."

"Is this an American-based organization?"

"Well, yea, but the whole process is about leveraging values and relationships, which really isn't American-centric at all. If you think about it, the American 'results over relationships' business model is really just a 120-year aberration considering how many centuries companies have been doing business together. I think America may be coming around to a more European model in terms of the value and reliability of relationships, but with an added focus on developing and nurturing them and not just haphazardly using them to get the next opportunity. Also, I don't know if you know this, but our own Ben Franklin was perhaps the original value-based networker, or Networlder.

"He grew the democratic foundation in the U.S. by bringing people of virtuous values together in small circles around the country and then helping those circles connect and share information, encouraging individuals and groups to leverage their collective power to make positive changes happen faster."

"Well," replied Dawn, smiling. "If it was good enough for 'ol Ben at the nation's founding, it certainly should be good enough to take us through the next century! I'd love to be in Vienna."

Darryl bent and gave her two quick kisses on the cheeks. "Buenos Noches."

"You too," she replied. The door shut quietly as he left.

Dawn sat down on the couch and started to think about her board meeting the next morning and how she planned to make sure she gave and also what she might ask for in exchange. Then she rose and went to her laptop. She had some changes to make to her presentation.

✳

When Dawn arrived at the office the next morning she was prepared for the worst. The people in the office were scurrying about, printing and copying final preparations for the board meeting at 10 a.m. Dawn dropped her bag on her chair, extracted her folder and copies of her presentation she had finished late the prior night, and strode directly into Francios' office.

"Here's what I have," she said, and dropped the packet onto his cluttered desk. He looked up in surprise.

"What do you mean?" he asked, with a look of puzzlement on his face.

"I mean this," Dawn replied, pointing to the presentation. "Maybe I was a little hasty in my judgment on the timing of your campaign. I was thinking last night and perhaps there is a way for us both to help the company."

She opened the presentation to page four and flipped it right-side up for Francios to read. "I believe the market research is correct and that your new services and the marketing muscle behind them are premature." She could see the beginning of a scowl starting to form on his face.

"But," she added, "I think I have a solution that will allow us to test the market with the new services, in a sort of 'pilot' phase...and then pull back if we don't get the response we need."

Francois leaned a little closer and read the recommendations in the presentation. A tiny smile formed on his face. Dawn continued quickly.

"Now by no means does this mean that I will recommend a full rollout of your new services. However," she added, "I believe that we can test the market and minimize exposure to the shareholders by executing in this area," she flipped a page.

"And here," she turned another. "And here. That way we'll let the market tell us early enough that we can pull back the campaign with minimal risk...or accelerate it and take advantage of a first-mover situation."

She stepped back from his desk and glanced into his face. After Darryl had left last night, she had thought long and hard about what he had said. It finally dawned on her that 'giving' in some cases meant no more than stubbornly sticking with an opinion she thought was right. By re-crafting her messages into an 'exchange', she could achieve her goals, voice her opinion, but do it in a way that left open the opportunity for benefits across a number of areas in case she was wrong, or just partially right.

Exchanging with Francois was difficult; she found him incredibly hard to work with (the perennial French-American conflict), but personalities never counted, only results did. And more important, she knew that the marketplace always has the last say; and market indicators, despite their accuracy, are still like driving an automobile by looking through the rear-view mirror. The information may be accurate, but it's aged even before it is printed. And in the 21st century, markets changed at lightening speed making it impossible for anyone to keep up with ease.

Dawn looked into Francois' face and saw the growing gleam in his eyes. He rose from behind the desk and stepped around to approach her. He allowed himself a small smile, as genuine as was possible for him, and led her to the door. "Let's go," he said. "The board is waiting." Dawn took a deep breath and let him accompany her to the boardroom.

✳

*"If a man digs a pit, he will fall into it.*
*If a man rolls a stone, it will roll back on him."*
Proverbs 26:27

# CHAPTER 7
## The Taker

Marie exited the O'Hare terminal with her bags in both hands, looking desperately for a taxi amidst the afternoon Chicago downpour. The man standing beside her offered her some protection under his umbrella while they both waited at the sidewalk outside Terminal Five.

"You look like you've had a long day," the man said to Marie.

Marie looked up at a distinguished grey-haired gentleman standing next to her. He smiled at her with his brilliant blue eyes.

"Yes," Maried replied. "I've been travelling since early this morning and I have to go directly to my office now for a meeting."

"Oh, what kind of a place would make you do that?" he asked with real compassion.

Marie paused before answering, and then realized that the truth of this stranger's comment rang true.

"You're right," she answered with a tone of resignation. "It's just the nature of business today it seems."

"I worry about you young business people today. I wonder how my kids are going to fair in a marketplace where you are all competing so aggressively."

"Things are changing," Marie said. "I've just recently had the opportunity to participate in a business optimization session overseas. The good news is that there are a growing number of people who understand the importance of developing networks of relationships with people who focus more on values first and goals second."

"That sounds interesting," he said, watching the taxis pull aside one by one. "What values are you referring to?"

"A number of different values. For example," Marie replied, "my number one value is integrity. If I am in alignment with that value on a daily basis, then there will be things that I do or don't do each day that will clearly show that integrity is one of my core values. By having chosen integrity as one of my core values, I am able to more quickly make choices that lead to better outcomes. In the case of my company, this meeting I'm attending is going to be run by a young man named Jim with whom I've had conflicts in the past.

"His goal is financial gain or power over others and I can't imagine what values he has to support those goals. What I do know is that he works for the Marketing department, with whom I've also had some conflicts, and I'm going to be at odds with him because we come from two totally opposite beliefs on what it takes to be successful."

"This guy sounds like he's only interested in what he can 'get' out of any deal." The man turned and noticed that a taxi had just drawn up beside them.

"You understand," Marie quickly said as she waved him to the taxi first. "It's all about givers, takers, and when you get really good, exchangers. This guy is definitely a taker."

The man smiled and kindly offered Marie the taxi in front of them both. Marie politely declined, as he had been waiting longer. He then said, "The best way to build an opportunity sounds like when you get good enough to be an exchanger. So how about we share this taxi downtown and benefit from this exchange because we both seem like we're good exchangers?"

Marie looked closely at him, smiled, and accepted the offer. As she passed her bag to the driver to put into the taxi's trunk, she reflected on the conversation and smiled to herself. Darryl would be pleased.

※

Marie took a deep breath, clutched her notes more tightly to her side, and stepped through the door into the conference room. Janet and Jim were already seated. Mark and Erin were both at the coffee machine in the corner of the room. A number of other executives were scattered about around the table. She noticed after a moment that not a single member of her team was in the room. She diverted her entrance and walked directly up to Mark.

"Wasn't the emergency e-mail that I received on the plane sent to anyone else on my team?" she asked. Jim stepped quickly up to Marie and interjected. "Oh, Marie, didn't anyone tell you that this meeting only requires your participation."

"Why is that?" she asked. "I thought we were working in partnership with each other on this initiative?"

Mark stepped forward, noticing Marie's discomfort, and said. "It was Jim's decision that we hold this meeting today and that no one else from your team be required to attend because he has a solution that he thinks you will be pleased with." Marie looked at Jim with a mixture of anger and bewilderment. She was starting to get a strange feeling about the meeting. "Jim, just what kind of solution are you referring to? The one I recommended over the phone from Madrid, or something different?"

Jim avoided Marie's direct gaze and answered, "Let's just sit down and start the meeting. I'm sure we'll all come to a decision that will make everybody happy."

With that, Marie pulled herself together. It was not going to benefit her to show how angry she was at Jim's obvious manipulations. She knew that it would be much better to first show acquiescence on any minor points and present her position strongly on the key issues of the campaign. The group quickly seated themselves. Jim looked questioningly at Mark, who nodded an ok for him to start the meeting. Jim rose and walked to the head of the table.

"Thank you all for coming. I want to take this opportunity to share an exciting new development I was able to secure regarding the launch of our new initiative to attract the thirty-somethings in Madrid for our new offerings. Just yesterday morning I secured one of the top Spanish rock singers in Madrid that has been at the head of the charts for the year and has agreed to headline our campaign. And the best news is that he agreed to our budget because we 'enticed' him with an opportunity to be introduced into the American music scene through one of our corporate contacts. So whether we actually deliver on that or not doesn't matter. The important thing is we got the deal the way we need it in order to keep corporate off our backs and to penetrate the key market we've targeted in Spain."

Marie sat there in shock. She hadn't anticipated this at all. She didn't realize how much of a taker he could be. For one, Jim had agreed with her on the phone from Madrid a few days earlier that they would co-present the solution and garner joint glory. For another, here was Jim creating a totally separate solution without involving her at any level. He must have originated this possibility days ago.

Plus, Mark and she had agreed weeks ago to let the market determine whether the thirty-something or the teen-market was the right one to target. Her solution had satisfied both of their objectives. This move by Jim could only mean that Jim had deliberately been working on his own plan when she and he had talked about the solution she had arrived at with Darryl in Spain.

Again, she knew better than to push back too hard, too soon. She opted instead to ask a question. "Jim, how does this help us clarify which market has the highest potential for our offering?"

Jim pursed his lips as he considered the question, and replied. "This is exactly what corporate has been asking us to do for months. We have focused on the customers with the most money, highest transaction volumes, and best credit worthiness appropriate for a new product introduction"

Mark was feeling increasingly uncomfortable with Jim's comments and interrupted him immediately. "What I think Jim is trying to say is that we leveraged your idea, Marie. He suggested that the teens are the strategic leverage points for us and managed to get the deal at cost. The difference in savings will go directly to the bottom line of the budget and will give us more cushion for the launch."

Marie started to get warmed up. "Mark, my team has done compelling research in the Spanish marketplace to help us enter and grow the market quickly. The teens are not yet loyal to any Spanish carrier or product and have a strong acceptance of American services. I think that focusing on just one market is risky, which is why I thought we agreed to a co-market approach."

Mark waved Jim back to his seat. He realized that this meeting had not gone the way he'd planned. Thinking quickly back on his discussions with Jim over the previous three weeks, he realized now that he'd not communicated effectively. Jim and he held similar ideas around the importance of marketing within the company, but not so similar values and ways in which they could achieve those goals.

As Mark watched Jim regain his seat, he reflected on the discussion that Marie and he most recently had, where Marie had seemed excited about some new way in which she thought they could work together. Mark was a born skeptic. But, he was always willing to listen to a good idea, and Marie was someone who always seemed to do things purposefully. Things that she had embraced had always ended up adding value to the company after being implemented. For example, the time she had worked with the public sector in creating an alliance between certain public agencies had resulted in a major contract with the government to be the primary supplier for law enforcement agents.

Jim's behavior made Mark think that this meeting was a bad idea. It was becoming apparent that Marie was not happy with the decisions they'd made in her absence. Upon reflection, Mark realized that perhaps his team had overstepped their bounds. He glanced at Jim and decided to take more control over the meeting.

"Marie, I apologize," he said. "It's apparent to me that Jim has not communicated with you as extensively about this as he inferred. I understood that you two had spoken and that you had agreed to support us in this decision to take advantage of the deal potential of the Madrid rock star and leverage it to penetrate the thirty-somethings market there. Since that is obviously not the case, I think we need to seriously review both options before moving forward."

Marie looked at Mark and smiled appreciatively. She then looked at Jim and said, "What I would advocate now is for us to look at our relationships with our respective groups and ask ourselves the question, 'Which one offers Calcom Telecommunications the best partnership for leveraging Europe.' You know that when we get done with Spain, we'll need to move into a number of other countries very quickly. Our ability to leverage this investment across multiple countries is critical.

"As you've seen from the research in front of you that my team compiled, our UK cross-over artist has top-10 appeal in all major European countries, while the group from Madrid merely has top ranking in Spain and Portugal. If the real bottom line is Europe, then doesn't that speak to the solution that delivers a broader potential across our markets?"

Jim did not respond. He just sat there staring at Marie. She could see he was not going to give up his ground and therefore she needed to make the next move to break the stalemate that was emerging. She rose to her feet and politely said to the entire group, "Thank you Mark, Jim, and the rest of you for sharing with me your ideas. I appreciate them. I know we have to make a decision quickly, but we agreed to work as a team and I don't see that happening today. Therefore, I will wait for you to come back to me with your decision as to how we can proceed when we clearly haven't come to a consensus." Then, before anyone in the room could utter another comment, Marie waltzed out, leaving behind a very bewildered team leader and his group of equally bewildered employees.

※

*"At times to be silent is to lie...you may win,*
*but you will not convince."*
Miguel de Unamuno, Spanish Writer, 1936

# CHAPTER 8
## Darryl's Evangelism

"Here's what I mean," Darryl said, standing up abruptly.

He strode forcefully to the front of the room. Around the well-used mahogany table in Danatech's Palo Alto headquarters sat before him fifteen of the dourest looking executives he'd seen in quite some time. No doubt they should be dour. Over the weekend, a competitor had 'trumped' them, and now Darryl had to attend this emergency meeting on the west coast. It was Monday morning and exactly one month since he'd returned from holiday in Spain. Darryl was still excited about applying the Networlding model he learned overseas.

Nevertheless, this was a crisis. Danatech had heard Saturday on CNN that a major competitor, JGStar, was coming out with a fourth generation technology that was significantly more advanced than their own. Everyone was up in arms. The Chief Strategy Officer had been called to the office Sunday morning and fired for not being aware of the competitive situation. Two of the major institutional investors had called the chairman personally on Sunday afternoon, and Bruce, the energetic CEO whom Darryl knew well, was avoiding all contact with the press until after this meeting. They were in 'siege mentality' and there was an unavoidable analyst conference scheduled for early in the afternoon.

No one was happy. Not only was it likely that this unforeseen move by their chief competitor would freeze future sales in their pipeline until they responded with their own enhanced product (at least six months of product development and testing away, even if they worked at 'internet speed'), but also there was a real risk of existing contracts being cancelled or suspended by some of their largest corporate customers here and in Europe as each of them ran the numbers and looked at the economics associated with switching technologies. Revenue and earnings projections from Friday's staff meeting looked woefully out of date

Darryl had been called on Sunday afternoon just as he was preparing to leave his flat in Florida. Bruce, his old client, asked him in a panic to fly to Palo Alto Sunday evening. When Darryl hung up the phone, he knew it was serious. Never before on a call, no matter the importance, had Bruce not recounted ad nauseum additional facts about his shipboard experiences steaming up to Alaska during the years he was working his way through university.

Darryl knew the stories by heart and could even parrot them back to Bruce on occasion. It was almost a private joke between them when Bruce sprinkled those stories, lessons learned, and the paltry amount he was paid for the 7x16 week he worked shipboard, into their business conversations. But on this call, there was no joking.

Bruce was one of the executives whom Darryl had done significant (and successful) strategy work for in the past, and now he was in trouble. As he quickly packed a travel bag, Darryl grumbled to himself that this was one result of his 'network' that didn't excite him all that much. Especially with the National Basketball Association basketball finals underway. He'd scraped together tickets to the game, which was on the east coast, and had to hand them off to friends at the airport before boarding his flight. Their malicious grins stuck with him all through the pasty pasta dinner on the plane. Today, as he approached the front of the boardroom, he was still seething a bit at the change in his plans over the last sixteen hours, but he knew he couldn't let his friend down.

Despite the disappointment of missing one of the American pastimes he enjoyed most (i.e., professional sports where there actually was something important at stake), on the flight over he'd done some serious thinking about the dilemma facing the company and his old client. He wasn't a product development specialist, although he was fairly well-versed in most technologies, and certainly well-versed in the financials of the company before him.

On the plane he struggled to decide what messages he would deliver to the executive team. Finally, an answer gravitated to him at 36,000 feet. Networlding. The more he thought, the more he felt that this was a good situation to try to shape company skills and behaviors to meet this crisis and the next and the next. If this wasn't a 'strategic inflection point' to quote *Only the Paranoid Survive* by Intel executive Andy Grove, Darryl couldn't think of what one was. This might even be a case of "The Innovator's Dilemma' to quote Clayton Christianson's excellent treatise on the subject. Or even…Darryl stopped. He had enough problems without inventorying all the old '90's business books that rose in his mind. He grinned to himself. Although upset at missing the game, this kind of crisis is what got his blood pumping.

Jotting down a few notes and diagrams on paper and into his laptop, he sketched out his approach to the meeting and even managed to get a few hours sleep on the flight. In the morning when he awoke, he reviewed his notes and actually whistled his way into work. For a crisis, he felt amazingly at ease. He reached the white board in the front of the room, casually selected a marker from the tray, and turned to face the group.

"This is not a technology issue," he said, paraphrasing his friend Marie. "This is a people issue." He drew a number of diagrams across the whiteboard. "Now I'm going to take you through these pictures. You all know me; we've worked together in the past. You know that my style is not to dominate a discussion, but to facilitate it. In this case, I really want you to listen to what I am saying. We have five hours before the press conference. What I want to do is not just help you decide what you will say to the street, but help you get positioned so that this

NEVER happens again." The look in the eyes of the executive team was enough for him to go on. They would listen.

"I'm also not the most compassionate or 'high-touch' person in the room," he said. They all chuckled at that, remembering that Darryl had delivered a powerful strategic plan a few years back that had delivered many millions to the bottom line. One of the key tenants of the plan was a complete re-tooling of a few critical departments. This had resulted in thousands of people being forced to undergo a rather ruthless upgraded training program or face promotion restrictions, raise limits, and even severance. It was the right thing to do but was traumatic to an organization that had started twenty years earlier with pizza parties, kids' days, and a general good-fellow culture.

Darryl continued. "I'm not the highest-touch person here, but I've seen the inside of a lot of boardrooms in crisis. And I've seen a lot of operating models fail because the companies didn't utilize their most important 'capital' properly. I'm not talking about technology capital, brand capital, financial capital, or even intellectual capital. Those are static assets with static costs and returns. I'm talking about human capital – the one thing in an organization that we cannot predict, measure, or really monitor...but we can nurture, expand, and leverage it. What I'm going to talk about now is beneficial to all the individuals that make up the most important asset in your company – to you and the shareholders as well. It is also the single most important thing that you need to focus on now to deal with this crisis."

He turned to the first of his diagrams on the whiteboard and began to speak. "Here we have a simple graphical representation of your company, with a typical structure. You have departments focused on certain business functions, like R&D and Sales & Marketing, and you have organizational levels. Read Hammer again to remind yourselves why functional organizations have trouble and why process-aligned companies communicate so much better when the 'storms of change' hit. As you recall, this was my view a few years ago." He couldn't resist looking at the HR director who had squashed his ideas to reorganize earlier.

71

"And within this depiction of your organization we can see the borders that inhibit you from quickly 'operationalizing' key decisions up and down within a functional area, as well as across functions. Everyone stays in their organizational 'box' – no one reaches out upwards…or downwards effectively. Everything is delegated and separately 'housed' in the company, and you have performance metrics to reinforce these borders. This is what I call the 'cheese pizza' model. Everyone is in their 'piece' and no cheese superstars cross borders, because there is no organizational incentive to do so. And you wonder why JGStar beat you to the market." He looked at them and saw them gazing intently at his diagram.

"What I'm trying to say is that you cannot be in a 'fast curve' industry like technology with this kind of alignment and expect to ever have first mover advantage, sustain it over time, or defend against someone else's. These functional 'islands' are left over from the eighteenth century. They really need to go. It didn't hurt you in the beginning because you had an innovative idea and speed to market was your objective. Now, you need to reinvent yourselves or you're going to get left behind." He looked at them with a spark of his old fire. He was getting warmed up.

"The interesting thing is that your people already have broken this model. Recognize one thing. Your people don't care about your structure. Sure, some are content inside their little slice. But the ones that are not have already built spontaneous circles of interest throughout the company. They've already reached beyond the borders and connected with other like-minded individuals. Whether you call them lunch groups, circles of interest, or anything else, the issue you have is that there is no reason for these informal networks to be aligned with your business objectives. Why should they? Circles are forming in a haphazard manner, based on values that may be important to individuals, but may have little to do with helping the company prevent what happened this weekend." He looked at them. They were quieter than he had ever seen an executive team on a Monday morning.

"Your first job is to understand which naturally occurring circles are being formed within the four walls of this building, and identify those that are most important to 'cluster' and align with corporate objectives. Once clustered, and you can expand and nurture existing circles or even help form new ones to assist individuals in identifying and capturing opportunities for satisfaction and success.

"Now, you need to apply some criteria to these natural clusters. I will not say apply 'structure' because structure inevitably stifles innovation and individuality. And you don't and really can't 'own' these circles, you just want to leverage them. You need to design criteria to help you identify and align the circles that will create the best vehicle through which you can harness all this human capital and leverage these individuals who are reaching out, who are already 'wired' to connect with others of like-minded values or interests."

Darryl moved in front of another diagram that he had drawn. "Now we get to the market. Finally, some of you are thinking! Well, you know I think most companies are far too worried about intellectual property rights, firewalls, and command and control. You can see by the bold line around the picture that no matter how you re-align, no matter how you encourage circles of interest, you still have a thicker outside border between you and your customer and between you and your competitors than is healthy.

"Trust me when I say that I know for fact that more vital information between competitors is leaked between friends over a beer than was ever leeched out of a corporate database. Intellectual property has a half-life of weeks or months in your industry. Like it was in the beginning for you, it's still speed-to-market that differentiates. It's consumer awareness and a smart value proposition that builds share-of-mind and a sustainable first-mover advantage. Leveraging your people, your human capital inside the company is not enough.

"You have one more border to breach. And to breach it you need management's resolve. It has to come from you. This border is too thick to conquer without strong support and commitment from management.

"With an internal series of aligned circles of interest, a supportive corporate culture, and management's resolve to encourage and leverage these naturally occurring communities of interest, you now have the capability to extend outside yourselves and begin to tap into the marketplace itself, beyond these thick borders that surround your company.

"Thousands of people in your company have relationships with peers outside the company. These outside relationships will naturally be between people with like-values, and most likely with people who work for your competitors, your customers, your suppliers. So the naturally occurring clusters of interest inside your own organization, which you just need to identify and nurture a bit more, become prototypes of the naturally occurring clusters of interest outside your company.

"What this effectively means is that you 'extend' the enterprise and begin to integrate it into the best thinking in the market. And when you dissolve your 'levels' and 'silos' that prevent effective communications and decision making, you'll suddenly have access to real market data, innovative ideas, creative alternatives, etc., and it will flow through the organization like a virus. You won't know what hit you. All of us in this room don't care a 'whit' about being the 'technology company of the future' as stated by our vision statement. What we care about is our mission statement which is 'to provide outstanding products and services to our customers along with outstanding opportunities for our people'. With this concept, we can do both, and we will realize our vision in the process."

Darryl took a deep breath as he stood in front of the group. "Now I may sound like a Chicago Bears fan cheering on the Green Bay Packers, but this isn't just an ordinary change I'm talking about. This will fundamentally alter everything about your company. Utilizing an individual set of principles for people to willingly communicate and collaborate their aspirations and interests through value-based circles is one of the powerful tools you'll need to turn this company around.

"What I'm suggesting is essentially Networlding – a pre-thought out transformational process by which you support and leverage the naturally occurring 'circles' within, across, and most important for your product development and future 'speed to market' capabilities, outside your organization."

Darryl looked hard at the attentive executives before him and pointed at the diagram. "You as a management team have a fiduciary responsibility to encourage and nurture these individuals. Once you decide to do so, as this diagram shows, you will begin to be far more interested in the 'informal' clusters of like-valued individuals in your organization than in the formal bureaucracy, reporting hierarchy, or organizational levels. What you need is a 'learning organization' capable of connecting inside and outside along lines of similar values and interests."

Darryl took another breath and then walked slowly back to regain his seat along the side of the table. There was a lengthy silence in the room. He took a sip of water and continued. "Now, with that said, how do we respond to JGStar and your analyst conference in," he looked at his watch, "three hours time?"

An icy silence ran through the room.

Bruce, the CEO, looked around the room and slowly spoke. "Darryl, I don't know quite what to say. I don't know if it's the crisis or the coffee, but I've never quite heard something like this before. It seems incredibly simple, yet we've blindly ignored our great people since shortly after we moved into these large offices five years ago and started playing with the big boys."

Bruce glanced around the table. The director of HR was looking askance, his head down, shuffling his notes before him. The Chief Technology Officer was furiously writing notes, a gleam of excitement in his eyes. He got it. And a few of the others got it too.

The rest of the executives were in various stages of shock, disbelief, or dismay. Bruce stood up and walked to the front of the room. There was a different spring in his step than that which Darryl had observed earlier. He was a large man with a warrior mentality, and had seemed beaten and stressed a few hours ago when they had convened the meeting. Now a bit of the 'killer' that had taken the company from a few tens of millions in revenue to billions was back. He squared his shoulders and faced the group.

"Darryl, I want you to come with me and Bill, our Chief Financial Officer, and help us craft the message to the analysts. You, Arthur," he pointed to the CTO, "and Josephina, and Matt. I want the new prototype schedule cut in half. I want an operational demo by the end of the month."

Without pausing to see the look of excitement in Josephina or Matt's faces, or the look of anxiety in Arthur's, he continued. "And you three," he continued to point, "I want the complete spec package around JGStar's product launch and any alliance partners they have, whatever is publicly available, on my desk by five o'clock." He continued to bark out orders until everyone had received their instructions. The meeting broke quickly as the executives scrambled off to their offices, mobile phones already in hand, urgently communicating to their staffs.

Darryl gathered up the sparse notes that he had written on the plane the evening before and walked over to Bruce. His thoughts were settling down. His message seemed to hit home with the executive team. He had been worried that he'd been indoctrinated or lulled into these circles of interest, this Networlding concept, in a moment of weakness while relaxing on holiday. Good ideas on holidays always seemed to evaporate when he returned to the business trenches and the reality of hard problems facing hard people. But the evidence he'd seen in the room this morning gave positive proof that his fears were unfounded.

He never thought, even with his own relationship-oriented style, that he'd stand up in front of a company in crisis and sell them futures when the market was about to short the stock. He grimaced to himself, and then sighed. It was the right answer. He was sure of it. Both for the individuals locked in their home-grown, haphazard ways of networking and communicating, and for a company stocked with such talented people waiting to unleash their ideas, talents, and relationships. There was plenty of hard work to do to deal with the immediate crisis, but the seeds for future innovation and growth had just been sown. And they seemed to have taken root well.

Bruce clapped his hands on Darryl's shoulder with a wry grimace, with half a smile, and half an expression of pain. "C'mon, Darryl. Let's see what we can do about the wolves at the door." With that, they walked out of the room, down the hallway and into his office, closely followed by the CFO, who had grabbed his papers and was hustling after them.

"Would you like some coffee?" he asked Darryl when all three of them had been seated in his office.

"Yes, thanks." Darryl replied. While Bruce was getting the attention of his executive assistant to fetch them some coffee, Darryl looked around the office. It had been nearly a year since he had last been at this client's office and there were notable changes – the most notable being the dishevelled desktop and numerous whiteboards scattered about the room. It looked more like a war-room than an executive's office.

Darryl turned to face Bruce, who was placing the phone back into its cradle. "Sylvia will be here shortly with a fresh pot," Bruce said.

Darryl nodded.

Bruce continued: "Now," he settled back into his chair, "why don't you debrief Bill and I a bit more so that we are ready for the analysts. How much of what you said in there is immediately applicable to the current situation and how much is 'nice to have' over the rest of the fiscal year?"

Darryl looked over the table and grinned. "Well, you can't change overnight. What you want to do, once we prep and get through this analyst meeting in a few hours, is to schedule a webcast to the organization for first thing tomorrow morning. After the analyst meeting we'll lay out the key tenants of your webcast and communicate directly to the organization the attack strategy you'll take to respond to the JGStar threat. I think you should offer up a few IDs and passwords to those analysts who are likely to be 'friends of the firm' and let them clandestinely tune in. It may help in the media over the next few days if they get a direct read on your action plan." Darryl paused.

"That's a wonderful idea," said Bruce. "It's been a long time since I took the reins in terms of directly communicating with everyone. In the old days, we'd all get together once a month off-site and I'd go through the current production, sales, and market situation." He paused and pursed his lips together. "Perhaps it's time to get back some of our old culture."

Darryl looked thoughtful for a moment, glanced at the CFO who was quietly listening, and then spoke. "Bruce, I'm not sure which parts of your old culture will help or hurt you right now. Some of the things you can do with a small company in terms of innovation and communication can be very destructive in a company of your size. Yet, certainly there are some cultural components and aspects of entrepreneurial boundarylessness that you could certainly have used over the last six months as JGStar was getting ready to eat your lunch.

"I know a few years ago I was pushing you hard to re-align the company along customer segments, with shared services for IT, human resources, and finance to support different customer-facing, P&L responsible business units. I think if you had done that, you may have been more sensitized to the market, your competitive intelligence and research efforts may have have given you earlier indicators, and you may have been closer to your customers to know what unarticulated needs they had, and what JGStar was doing to meet those needs."

Darryl glanced intently into Bruce's face. "I think if there is anything I'd recommend right now it would be for you to personally step up and become the voice of the company again – both to the street and to your people. The time for individual leadership has returned. I know it's your passion and your strength. I suspect you've taken a back seat to the great talent you've brought into the organization over the last few years. And I know you're a strong supporter of structured organizational design and proper performance incentives and business metrics to ensure all the functions and people are integrating correctly. But I hope I've shown you today that the old model of categorical organizational design and performance management systems is still based on eighteenth century principles, even if the concepts are prettied up with twenty-first century consulting-ese. So your support for organization and structure has prevented you from being at the center of the most important organic 'circle' that the company has – the leadership circle. If the street is going to have confidence in this company, and if your people are to maintain their morale and commitment over the coming year, it's going to have to come from you."

Bruce looked thoughtful for a moment. Then he glanced directly into Darryl's face. "You're right. I have taken a back seat. Maybe I've been reading too many business books and not paying attention to my gut enough." He had a pained look on his face. "But when you start a small company with close friends and a few years later suddenly find yourself in charge of a multi-billion dollar concern, then all the shareholders and families who are relying on you weigh on your mind. The difference in visibility is tremendous. I have to be sure to make the best business decisions, and I'll tell you, I try to learn as much as I can from the Andy Grove's and the Jack Welch's of the world to ensure I do that."

Darryl interrupted. "You know what I think, Bruce? I think if you asked Andy Grove or Jack Welch how many business books they read each year, you could count them on the fingers of one hand." There was a stunned look on Bruce's face. Darryl continued. "These guys are just like you and me. The difference is they've uniquely leveraged the leadership skills they have to gain success in the market. But their success isn't yours or mine. And their techniques aren't the same either. They can't be, because leadership is an individual thing.

"Leadership is a gift that everyone has uniquely and that needs to be unwrapped uniquely as well. For some, they figure out how to pull off the ribbon, rip off the paper, and open up the box when they are eight years old. And they're the ones in the teenage investor clubs, drama leads, sports captains, and later on in positions where they can hone their gifts directly in university and the market.

"For many others, it takes a while to learn that they can be leaders, whether it's visionary leadership, or pragmatic leadership, or any other of the dozens of types of leaders that I'm sure you've read business books on." Darryl grinned mischievously at Bruce and continued. "After all, not all our families and the environments in which we grew up help us reach our peak potential. All of us have weight we carry, obstacles to overcome. Being born to wealthy parents can be a greater burden for some people than being born into urban poverty. The point is that you get no 'points' for the length of the journey you take. You get points for being where you need to be in the world when you need to be there. For some people, they experiment for years in opening up their leadership gifts. Some never succeed. Some read so many books by so many people that they couldn't possibly apply all the techniques they've read in any intelligible way. They actually add layers to their gift, making it harder to open than ever.

"And that's my point. There is no intelligible way of learning leadership skills and behaviors. You can communicate ideas and examples and techniques in books and seminars and generate awareness. But individuals cannot learn leadership from the outside in. Adoption is fundamental to learning, and adoption is an inside-out process. Adoption is as individual as what flavor ice cream you like and why. Depending on the journey you've taken in your life; whether it's from single-parent poverty or the addictiveness of early wealth, how you adopt, how you unwrap your gifts of leadership, and how you apply them is 100% you. That's why I think you should stop reading and start doing.

"I think you should get up in front of those analysts and take back this company. Be Danatech. You already are in your heart and mind. Bring that out and re-establish it in everyone's mind. I know you well enough to know that if you do this, it will buy you the time in the market and the passion in your people to counter-attack and defend your business against JGStar." Darryl stopped.

Bruce looked at him with an expression of gratitude and respect. "Darryl," Bruce said, "I think you've just earned yourself a spot on our permanent market advisory board."

Darryl looked dismayed. "Bruce, thank you very much, but I really don't want the position. What I want is to see you start to execute the way I know you can, and the way you used to when you had your pizza parties and kids days. This isn't silver bullet advice; it's just the only way I know for you to be you, and to be successful being you. What I said in the boardroom I said because I know you are the kind of leader who would support and nurture those circles of interest and find innovative ways of leveraging them to benefit you in the marketplace. I didn't come here today to be invited to sit on a board; I came because I genuinely believe in you and wanted to help."

Bruce looked at him again and shot him a genuine smile of appreciation. At that moment, Sylvia, his executive assistant, finally entered with a tray of coffee and set it carefully on the corner of Bruce's desk. The CFO shuffled his papers and looked at the both of them. Darryl crossed his legs and leaned back in his chair; he was feeling yesterday's long flight in his legs now. Bruce took out a sheaf of paper and began to write vigorously on it. After a few minutes of quiet, in which Darryl carefully sipped his coffee, Bruce tore off the few pages that he had written from the pad and passed them along to Darryl. Darryl set his coffee cup down carefully on the desk and read the pages carefully. It was Bruce's draft of his comments to the analysts. Darryl had to swallow twice and collect his emotions before he spoke. "It's perfect," he said. "It's perfect because it's you and only you. It's not Jack Welch or Andy Grove and what they would have done; it's what you are going to do."

Bruce looked at him with a fire starting to burn in his eyes. Not only was he excited about the idea of Networlding circles that Darryl had spoken of in the meeting, or the fact that he was going to step up to a more prominent leadership role, but he was excited about something else as well. He was excited that a single phone call to a trusted friend had, in less than twenty-four hours, completely changed everything about his life, his role in the company, and his approach to his career.

He now felt enormous appreciation of the fact that if he and Darryl had not shared common values and established a trusted relationship in the past, today would be turning out very differently. He turned back to the two sitting around his desk, and they began to work in earnest.

✳

*"It's all about relationship. When you connect with great people who have similar core values where you consciously collaborate, you live your life at a whole new level – a level where you can create incredible opportunities daily."*

Melissa Giovagnoli, co-author
*Networlding: Creating Relationships and Opportunities for Success*

# CHAPTER 9
## Marie's Evangelism

Mark was in earlier than usual that warm June morning.

He knew he had to see Marie and let her know that he had let Jim go. He had thought long and hard about what happened at their last meeting yesterday, where Jim, a very manipulative employee, had set Marie up for failure. Jim thought that making himself the "winner" in his boss's eyes would garner him a long-term gain at CalCom. Clearly Jim had no concept of teamwork or how human networks operate.

Suddenly Marie whisked by him carrying a bouquet of every color of rose he had ever seen or imagined. The flowers were wrapped in thick floral paper to protect her from the huge green thorns he could see protruding from some of the stems hanging at the bottom. This explosion of fragrance and color engulfed Marie as Mark walked into her. "Oh! Marie," he exclaimed, stifling a laugh under his breath from the change that had come over her in the past few weeks. "You look as though you just won a beauty contest!"

"Really?" Marie asked looking at Mark as though she had no idea as to what he was talking about. "What makes you say that?"

Mark looked at her with a puzzled expression on his face, "Marie, you have been working with me for more than five years now. You always show up on time, but not until the last few weeks have you ever arrived with more than a pensive look or scowl upon your face! What, may I ask, has been going on in your life that is giving you this new attitude?"

"Well, Mark, if you must know..." Marie looked around the hallway to see if there was anyone nearby. She wanted to have this discussion with Mark in private, but she was just brimming with joy that day because she had spent the night working on her Networlding action plan and decided how she was going to implement it in the office starting this day. But, she needed to be a bit less effusive she realized or she might come across as pushy when she started having conscious conversations with Mark and her team regarding the changes she decided to make in her office. "Mark, let's go into the East Conference Room and have ourselves a nice talk."

"Uh, oh," said Mark immediately. "I hope you are not going to bail on me. Marie, I need you here with this Madrid launch. You look too happy today and it is making me nervous. Are you planning to get married or something and leave us?"

Marie laughed more heartily than she had laughed in the last few weeks. She found herself recently laughing more often and more spontaneously than she had ever laughed. She also noted that Mark was glancing again at the big bouquet of roses she held gingerly in her right arm. "No, silly! I bought these roses for the people in my department. They represent a symbol of what is to come for my team – the things that I know will blossom from some of the things I learned over in Europe." As Marie spoke, she waved the bouquet in the direction of the East Conference room and marched in front of Mark down the hall. He followed quickly.

Once inside the conference room, Marie quietly shut the door behind them. She walked around the table, got herself a cup of tea, and sat down across from Mark who had already seated himself and was still looking at her anxiously. She took her time dipping her tea bag into her cup, adding a slice of lemon as she always did, and then, taking a sip of her tea. She looked up and smiled. "Mark, you know me well enough by now to know that I don't pull any punches when it comes to my work."

"That's for sure!" remarked Mark. A deep memory emerged in his mind of the time when Marie had challenged one of his employees to get a project completed within 48 hours or she would make sure that person never got the opportunity to work on another major project again with their joint team. Of course, she did the right thing. This person kept missing his deadline, and Mark had tried to diplomatically call the employee's attention to his poor performance. It was Marie who stepped in and made sure a gauntlet was thrown down, that was just tough enough to create a challenge rather than a threat. The employee rallied in this eleventh-hour challenge and the whole team congratulated both the employee and Marie for their performances.

Marie smiled at Mark's comment and continued on, "As I was saying, these roses," she gestured toward the roses now resting on the conference table, "these roses represent our relationships here at Cal-Comm. We have a collective strength, just like the powerful fragrance these flowers create. We also, though, like these roses, have our many thorns that keep others from connecting with the beauty that we offer. In other words, we have people who have, for one reason or another, created thorns that keep others from having a rich, full experience working with them."

Mark didn't say anything. He knew Marie had much more to say and that she was just beginning. He waited for her to go on.

"Mark, my team, like your team, has got to start doing business differently. We have to pull our thorns off and get closer to one another. We have to become a mixed bouquet that has no thorns, and thus we can embrace each other in a more powerful way. We need to have conscious conversations with each other daily within our departments and between our departments that co-create great opportunities."

"And we don't do that now?" Mark asked honestly.

"Mark, you know that we are usually at odds with one another, whether it's your team working with you, my team working with me, or our teams working with each other." Marie commented candidly.

"So, how would this look?" Mark pushed back.

"It would look like you telling me, for example, what your core values are and then I share mine with you." She looked at him squarely in his eyes and continued. "For example, Mark, I would guess that one of your core values is trust. Am I right?"

"Well, of course you are right. I mean I only talk about it at every meeting I have spoken about trust with my people as well as in our joint team meetings," Mark responded quickly.

"Okay, and you either know or could guess that one of my core values is trust," Marie commented just as quickly.

"Well, I haven't thought about your core values, but if I would, I guess that I would put trust right near the top."

"Good. That's where we begin and end our conscious conversations where we talk about how our core values align or don't align with our current relationships. As our values do align we know that we are heading in a similar direction when we are working together, and that if we become more conscious of our commitment to our values, we can use our joint commitment to achieve our goals much faster and more powerfully. Like the roses, we look different but we hold the same fragrance. And, we can now pull away the thorns that separate us from embracing a better way of working together." She paused again and waited for Mark to absorb what she said. He sat with his chin resting on his right hand, obviously thinking about what she had said.

She took another sip of her tea and continued. "Mark, remember when Angela and I were working on a project a year ago that we thought could result in a co-authored article? We never got to that point. I know she wanted to do it, but when it came down to it I decided against it, but I didn't know why. Now I do... Angela's core values were very different from mine. She valued autonomy and financial gain, whereas I valued collaboration and trust. We were coming from two very different places."

Mark was starting to see Marie's point. "Ah," he replied. "Therefore, with Jim, who I must add we let go of yesterday, he did not have the same core values as mine so there was no way that we could leverage opportunities for ourselves."

Marie looked at Mark with just a bit of surprise mixed with an acknowledgement. "Yes, and while I am very sorry to see Jim go because he was a very good employee, his core values were also not in alignment with mine. As he worked with both of us, he was bound to continue creating conflict in the projects where we worked jointly."

"Marie, you have something here that I think can help us at Cal-Comm. How can we use it to leverage the other projects we are working on within say, purchasing, HR, or with our CIO? They both laughed at this last reference because Amory, their CIO, had a reputation for being difficult with every team with whom she partnered internally. She was all about processes and just couldn't see the human side of system rollouts."

"Well, Mark. I think we have a challenge with some people more than others; however, if we apply some of the principles of Networlding – that's the process I learned about in Europe through my colleague Darryl – we can realize our goals faster and even achieve better results. We are still going to have to work at times with people whose values don't align with ours, yet we can leverage through those people whose values complement ours and buffer those others whose values conflict. So, for example, if Amory will allow it, which I am sure she would, we can work more with Anthony her director of e-business, to help us achieve our goals. Anthony, I am sure, does share our values; therefore, we can get our projects done faster and then deliver the results to Amory, whom I'm sure would be pleased not to have to be so involved with us as she has enough on her plate to keep her busy until two years from now!"

"Interesting strategy, Marie. I know that Peter Drucker has said often that the real work that gets done in any department is done outside of the traditional or documented process flows. I believe your Networlding offers that type of unconventional yet practical application of a more relationship-oriented process."

"Yes, it does, and it's more fun!" exclaimed Marie whose energy was again rising as she talked. "I realize that I have been working harder rather than smarter over the last few years. I am now focusing on relationships first, process second. This enables me to identify those people within and outside my organization who can best collaborate with me to achieve my department's goals. After all, isn't that what we are here to do?"

"Well, I believe that not even Jack Welch could say it any better!" Mark exclaimed. "Marie, I would like to learn more about Networlding."

"Well, it's easy Mark. A lot of what you are doing when you are in flow with a project involves Networlding principles. But even more so, we can bring Networlding within our company by starting circles within and between departments. This way we will all experience the power of the rose bouquet, coming together to create a melange of unique and creative individuals working together toward goals that can turn into transformational opportunities."

"Ah, Marie, now you have my full and undivided attention. Tell me more." Mark leaned forward with his hand still cupping his chin.

Marie picked up a marker and started writing on the flipchart positioned between them. She wrote down the following seven steps:

1. Start by identifying and sharing your top core values.
2. Determine who in your existing network are people who are 'ready, willing, and able' to have an exchange with you and who also hold similar values.
3. Continue to grow your primary circle to no more than ten people.
4. Throughout the process, develop powerful conscious conversations around the exchange.
5. Grow your relationships with your primary circle partners by setting up regular dynamic exchanges.
6. Brainstorm around co-creating transformational opportunities.
7. Leverage your relationships and opportunities for continued success by developing and practicing the Networlding process in the circles.

Marie and Mark continued to talk well into mid-morning, scribbling furiously on the flipchart and on the multi-colored post-its that lay on the conference table. They proceeded to stick the post-its over the entire surface of the table, creating a variegated landscape of colors that matched the colors of the roses that now lay on the mahogany side credenza overlooking a very sparkling Lake Michigan.

※

*"Know thyself – Nothing in Excess"*
Carved in stone above the entrance
of Apollo's temple at Delphi

# CHAPTER 10
## The Exchanger

Darryl was in his and Marie's shared office space early that morning getting ready for a circle meeting. This circle was by far his favorite, and he wanted to make sure he was prepared to answer the many challenging questions the members always seemed to ask. He was leafing through his guidebook when he heard someone pounding anxiously at his office door.

"Come in," he replied rather distractedly. He looked up to see Mathew, one of the circle's most ardent Networlders, standing in the doorway, looking rather dishevelled and flushed. He smiled and waved Mathew over to the chair in front of his desk.

The office was a small space he and Marie had shared these last six months since they'd decided to start their own Networlding circles and consulting practice together in Chicago. It was a beginning and they were making income from running the groups and facilitating their connections and growth. They didn't make much, but it paid the rent and they had a couple clients on the horizon ready to start circles within companies. He turned his attention to Mathew and said, "Hey, you look as though you just sprinted up the twenty flights of stairs! What's up?"

Mathew took a deep breath and launched into an excited burst of words, "I just got this great brainstorm preparing for a meeting this morning. I was busy at the gym running laps thinking about someone whom I have regularly networked with. Note that I said 'networked' and not 'Networlded'! Well, this guy I am referring to – his name is Brad – has been quite the taker. He calls me about every six months and it's always for something I can do for him. He never offers to do anything for me."

Darryl, who had been listening patiently, just smiled and nodded his head as a sign to encourage Mathew to continue. He knew better than to interrupt Mathew when he was thinking. It would take them too far off track so that they might not get back to the conversation for another half hour or so, and they had only about thirty minutes before the circle meeting today started.

"Well," Mathew continued, "as I was saying, Brad is so focused on making sure he gets his needs met that he seems to miss the part of supporting others and their needs. So, I had fallen asleep last night thinking about how to respond to Brad's latest six-month 'let's connect' email where he asked me to 'get him connected' to someone I have a good relationship with and I found myself dreaming about how to deal with him differently this time."

Mathew paused to look at Darryl to make sure he was still listening rather than laughing at his rather strange method for handling his concerns. Satisfied that he had an attentive audience, he continued, "Anyway, I was deep in sleep when the phone rang. It was my girlfriend, Jean, asking me to remember to come to her office after our circle meeting this morning. I realized that after I finished talking with Jean and lay back down to sleep that I had been dreaming about a great way to respond to Brad. You see, I had spent yesterday afternoon going through my guidebook in preparation for today's meeting." Mathew glanced over at Darryl, who was now leaning forward, his right elbow planted firmly on his copy of the Networlding guidebook, his fist pressed firmly against his cheek, his eyes glowing. Mathew smiled. Darryl had really developed an interest in his story.

He continued, "What I read was that 'The Exchange' in Networlding terms is about two people spending time together to go through the Seven Levels of Support with the goal of supporting one another's needs. As I understand it, it's a tool to help us get more from our professional relationships. I decided then to map out a Networlding Exchange Plan to use in my conversation with Brad." Mathew paused and pulled out a rather crumpled sheet of paper. He smiled, opened it up, and started reading from it.

"I started with the first level – emotional support. Here I wrote down that Brad, who I used to work with at Axiom, a web development firm where he was the VP of Business Development, was a very good rapport builder once we got in to see prospective clients. For example, I remember one time I took him to meet an executive in a major beverage company, and within five minutes he and the CEO were chatting away about their mutual love of art.

"I decided that I would praise Brad when I saw him regarding his ability as a way to start an exchange on that first level of emotional support. I would then ask him if he would share with me one thing he appreciates that I bring to the table with regards to building relationships with clients and prospects.

"Now for he second level, information support, I thought I would share with Brad that I do know two companies in his targeted vertical of health care that I heard were about to come out with a new product, and therefore might need web development assistance. Now I don't know people at this company, but I heard from a reliable source that the new Vice President of Marketing had said he wanted to explore new connections by developing a site to promote their new product line. In fact, he was looking for a new firm, and he wanted to give the business to a smaller, innovative one. I know Brad's firm would be great for this opportunity. In turn, I plan to ask Brad for the name of one company he might know of that would be interested in building alliances and that may need a good consultant like me to help him with that process.

"Third, I plan to share my knowledge support of proposal writing with Brad. This third level of support is really interesting because it emphasizes that someone's experiences or knowledge might be of value to another. It took me some time to figure out what experience I had that would be a useful to Brad. Then I remembered him sharing once that he was not good at writing proposals. I found myself thinking that someday I might share with Brad some of my proposals and show him some tricks I had learned from someone who was one of the best proposal writers I had ever seen.

"This morning, before coming over here, I pulled out a file with all my proposals and took one of the best to bring with me to my meeting with Brad this afternoon. In return, I plan to ask Brad to share with me his experience working with James Korning, the CEO of Hickman Electronics, one of the finest companies here in Chicago. I have been following James Korning's career for the past decade and would love to know more about him. I know Brad worked with his company, and from what he said, James plays golf at least once a week in the summer. I am going to ask Brad to see if we three might get together soon for a game.

"Fourth, when it comes to promotional support, I'm your guy. It's really my 'strong suit'. I can't help spreading the word about someone else when that person is someone whom I like and respect. I do like and respect Brad, and according to the guide-book, what I need to do here is tell Brad how I am going to talk about the things he does well and share his attributes with some of my key connections over the course of the next couple of weeks.

"The guidebook also adds that I should circle back around to Brad and let him know how people responded to me promoting him and that I should also request that Brad share things he recognizes I bring to the table – our value-propositions come to mind here, or at least what our Networlding partners see as our value propositions."

Mathew paused for a moment and looked at Darryl to see if he was following along. Darryl was still fixed just where he was when Mathew had started. Darryl gave Mathew a wide smile and waived his left hand for him to continue.

"Okay, now it gets exciting," said Mathew. He leaned in with both of his hands clasped to his knees. "I then come to the fifth level of support, wisdom support. Now this is tricky. I'm only in my thirties and I wondered if that would disqualify me."

He looked intently at Darryl. Seeing him shake his head to the right and left quickly encouraged him to keep goin. "Well, I figure that I have quite enough experience with developing alliance relationships that my exchange here should come in the form of three top strategies for forming great, long-term partnerships with one's clients. I know Brad would appreciate this. His firm, according to him, seems to acquire some great accounts, but then they seem unable to hold them past the one-year anniversary. My alliance experience has shown me that there are a few powerful strategies he can use to maintain those key relationships. In return, I would ask Brad to share his wisdom on pricing key account opportunities. I can always use some wisdom in this area, as I tend to price my services under what the market values for my services.

"On the sixth level of support comes what some may call 'the brass ring'. Here, according to the guidebook, we really can create for one another, in partnership, opportunities through transformational support. I spent more time thinking about the possibilities as to what this might look like in an exchange with Brad than any other support."

Darryl interjected, "That's just where you should be at this point. You are doing very well with this, Mathew. You've actually saved me lots of time and effort coming up with some concrete examples for today's session. You've come a long way in a short time. Thanks." Darryl looked at Mathew with genuine appreciation.

With that, Mathew grinned from ear to ear and launched off again at a rapid clip, "And so, with transformational support in mind I racked my brain to come up with something that was really out-of-the-box. Here, I thought about Brad's interest in kid's games. I thought about the work he had done at the Science and Industry Museum here in town. He had sold a project for his firm for them to create an online game for kids that helped them learn how to start and grow a business. I thought about my connection through my friend, Jim, to his friend Jill, who is the head of new product development at a board game company.

"It just so happens that he told me this week that Jill is looking on behalf of her organization to get into the creation of online games. So I decided that I would propose to Brad for his company and mine to have a conversation with Jill. She is here in town and I already called her and had set up an appointment to meet with her myself. Now, I think it would be good to bring Brad. In return, I will ask Brad to think about a similar opportunity. Again, according to our guidebook, rather than push Brad to do this, if I make a request for him to think about a similar opportunity over the next few days and to get back with me, it will create the potential for a transformational opportunity for both of us.

"The guidebook recommends that I wait to disclose my opportunity until we speak again. Overall, my goal should be to help him make better exchanges that support our respective goals.

"Finally, there's the seventh step of community support. This one's not easy because so many of us are operating from a position of survival. Networlding, as I have come to understand it, however, is about moving to a different place – a place of thrival."

"What is that?" laughed Darryl, throwing both of his hands up in the air. "Mathew, you are always coming up with great new words!"

Mathew laughed in unison with Darryl and said, "Thrival mode is about thinking beyond just getting by in life. It means we get up every day and think about how we can, with the support of others, get to a better, richer way of living. It's about not complaining so much, keeping focused on what does work, what you can do, and how you can work with other like-minded people like the Networlders to make this happen. That's how I see it. When we get to thrival mode we have become Nanosecond Networlders."

Darryl leaned back in his chair, folded his arms, and remarked, "I think you have something there, Mathew."

Mathew leaned forward even further and placed his hands now on Darryl's desk. "Yes! Here's where we realize the real benefit of Networlding. We accelerate our capability to improve and achieve our individual goals as well as the goals of the companies or shareholders for whom we work. Here, we find that life gets easier. The idea of community, from what I read in the guidebook, includes your work community, your family, friends, those who live near you, and even our world – our global community. At this level of the Networlding Support Exchange, there is a profound ripple effect.

"What you have created or co-created with other Networlders ripples through human networks all over the place. There is no end to the rapid and powerful effects of a good exchange. We are only limited in our possibilities by ourselves. But, because at their very core Networlders are naturally opportunity expansive, they are constantly looking for new and better ways to create continuous transformational opportunities for their community. And finally, in taking care of their community, they take care of themselves. There is great leverage here, great sustainability, and therefore, great fulfillment."

With that last statement, Mathew took a deep sigh and leaned back in his chair. He smiled at Darryl, who was not leaning forward but was concentrating on writing some notes on one of the pages in his guidebook. When there was almost two minutes of silence, Mathew cleared his throat, which made Darryl suddenly aware that he was being prompted to respond. Darryl quickly put down his pen and looked up at the clock. Realizing that the circle was about ready to start, he swung around the table, grabbed his guidebook with his right, and with his left hand patted Mathew on the shoulder.

He laughed again and said, "Thanks, Mathew. We are going to have to get you to facilitate a circle. I think you have what it takes. You certainly have the passion. That's one of the most important things when it comes to Networlding. Deming, the father of TQM and business quality, used to say, 'What gets measured, gets done.' In Networlding we say, 'What gets shared, gets done...as long as you have common values.' It's all about value-based Networlds, and you've shown you really understand that. "

"Thanks, Darryl," Mathew said humbly while he walked beside Darryl down the hall to the office conference room where their circle of ten was waiting to start their session. "Coming from you, that means a lot."

Darryl replied, "Well, I know that mastering The Networlding Exchange takes time. You have helped by providing a good example as to what an exchange might look like for two people in your line of business. Today, because we have senior executives who are out of work and other younger people just looking to develop their careers, we will expand on your framework to apply the principles to their interests and concerns. Let's go see what we can make happen in the next couple of nano-seconds!"

With that both, men turned the corner and marched into the conference room ready to share their insights.

*

# CHAPTER 11
## Future Net

"Marie, hurry up or we will be late for the meeting," shouted Darryl to a door that had been shut for more than ten minutes.

"I'll be right there," came Marie's voice from the other side of the tall oak door. The two were in Marie's loft in Chicago's West Loop, an area that was not just growing, but exploding with growth.

"What makes you think that you can be late when you are the one leading the circle?" asked Darryl, who absolutely hated to be late.

Just then, Marie appeared, looking very sexy. Darryl, who knew that he was not ready to make a commitment even after three years, said to Marie, "You look very nice today."

As usual, Marie smiled at him and said, "Ah, you are observant but nothing more my friend."

"What?" he inquired as he usually did when she had nailed his distinct and typical way of avoiding a conversation about their relationship.

Marie walked up slowly to Darryl and said, "Why don't we let the other peer facilitators take over the circle this morning so we can have ourselves a good talk." Marie gestured him over to her couch on the other side of the room.

Darryl hesitated for a moment. He was thinking only about business today, but Marie was quickly moving his attention away from his targeted plans. "Hmm. I don't know Marie."

He certainly didn't want to upset her. After all, she was the person who had supported him most in the world since they had reconnected on that serendipitous evening in Segovia when they both ran into Eduardo at Darryl's favorite restaurant. He thought further about the things that had transpired in their lives since that spring day.

Darryl reflected on these last few years. They had not only written a best-selling book together, but they had also created an incredibly successful consulting practice with lots of wonderful clients who had all become good friends to them both. He reflected especially upon his success with Danatech's turnaround, which is where it all came together. Within six months of his critical board meeting, the company had not only responded quickly and profitably to the JGStar threat, but they had also become the 'lighthouse' client for all of the Networlding concepts Darryl and the CEO had discussed that day.

Danatech had quickly established more values-based business relationships both inside the company and with all their major suppliers, had fostered innovation in a way that brought the corporate culture back to the entrepreneurial days of its origins, and invigorated their personnel to such a degree that they had matched and leaped past JGStar.

He then turned his thoughts to Marie's complementary success over the past few years. Marie stayed on with Cal-Comm for another year, helping them expand their products and services from Madrid throughout Europe, positioning them as one of the top providers in the marketplace. Networlding became an integrated part of Cal-Comm's leadership model, helping them establish a better mentoring program and also helping them better understand the differences in cultures necessary to launch and succeed in Europe and Asia. Marie played an instrumental role in that transformation.

As he reflected on the past, Darryl thought that perhaps today he had best let her have her way and see what happened. With Networlding now, he could easily afford to take a day off and actually enjoy himself a bit, even though it would be very hard to give up his need to always create challenges in his life.

He sat down on her beautiful Italian leather coach and waved her over. She came and sat down at his knees. Not a bad position for any man to be in, he thought.

He said, "Well, I guess since we have Harry co-running the circles these days, I'm sure he'll be okay without us. I'll just send him a data message and let him know we won't be there today."

Marie agreed with a twinkle in her eye. "Darryl, think about something that would really make you happy right now."

Darryl, of course, smiled right back at her and winked, "Well, Marie, I am always thinking about good things when I am with you."

"Darryl, I am not talking about anything too personal. I was just talking about things that make you happy in your personal life."

Darryl again smiled. He knew Marie too well. She was constantly trying to get him to talk about his commitment to her. Didn't she know that there would never be anyone else in the world for him except her?

Even though he couldn't make a commitment and they did not have any kind of personal relationship, he still was crazy about her. And, if it had not been for the fact that they were so busy working all the time, who knows what might be possible for them. But Darryl loved a challenge, and that superseded any other thoughts beyond friendship or companionship, and especially love. It was just that Marie and he had created so many wonderful things as a result of Networlding that he was inundated with new challenges, and that got him very excited.

But perhaps, just perhaps, he should be open to what she was saying now. He returned back to her sweet smile and beautiful face.

"Darryl, besides having great challenges every day that keep you happy in your work, and besides the fact that we have created many wonderful transformational business opportunities as a result of Networlding, what else makes you happy in your personal life?" Marie waited for his response.

"Well, Marie, to tell you the truth, you make me happy."

"Really? I am surprised, Darryl, as you don't seem to involve me in anything other than your professional life."

"Well, I am working on getting to that point someday," he replied candidly.

"Hmmm. And after two years you haven't gotten there yet?" Marie commented, not in any way trying to criticize Darryl's thought process, just calling it to his attention.

Darryl looked at Marie and started to shift his thoughts. Just like the Nanosecond Networlders had taught him, it only takes a second to change your life forever. And if anyone had changed his life forever, it was Marie. What if she had not knocked on his door two years ago in Madrid? He would not have gone down to the restaurant in Segovia that evening, choosing instead to eat his bread and cheese, his usual European dinner, alone in his chateau up in the attic surrounded by rotting magazines and books.

He would also probably not have reconnected with Eduardo. He would then not have learned of the Nanosecond Networlders or the Networlding circles. He would not have travelled to Paris and learned of the many different people from all over the world who were applying the useful principles of Networlding to improve their work and careers in general. He would not have found solutions to the issues in his workplace, nor could he have fully supported Marie with hers. He would also not have had the fun of helping Marie in her big launch in Madrid, which included him getting to play his guitar with the rock band he had connected her to through his buddy in the UK. He certainly would not have co-authored a book on Networlding with Marie and created this wonderful consulting practice with her that had them travelling around the world with some of the most powerful people in industries from manufacturing to entertainment. And he definitely would not have been featured in *Time*, *Fortune*,

*Forbes*, *Newsweek*, and *Fast Company* along with Marie. In other words, he would not have the incredible joy he had now working and being with someone he admired and trusted so much.

And now, he realized it. He had taken Marie for granted. He realized, suddenly, that all of his old models were just that. OLD. He realized that he needed to rethink these models.

After all, even though he loved reading every science fiction book on the planet, sometimes he got lonely. He had just forgotten, in his usually complicated and complex life, to involve Marie more. Obviously she was someone who deserved to be a bigger part of his life; yes, he spent time thinking about how to develop a more personal relationship with her, but then his day would get away from him or he would get distracted working on some project all night. He yawned just thinking about his days chocked full of activity.

Meanwhile, two years had passed! How did that happen? He looked again at Marie. He did think the world of her and wanted to be with her beyond his normal workday. He just had not thought about the two of them much. Now he started to think. Could they create some personal happiness together, and might that happiness grow into something even bigger and better than the relationship they currently had?

Could it be that even though he had had a wonderful committed relationship with his former girlfriend, that he could have some kind of relationship with Marie? What was commitment anyway? What did it look like? Did he ever ask Marie about that? Did he know her definition of commitment? He realized suddenly that he had totally left her out of his decisions. Although he valued her opinions, he had never asked her what she wanted.

Perhaps Marie had a construct, a model for a relationship they could have, that would not make him nervous, threatened, or mistrusting. Marie had come into his life with a different desire. She was not needy. She just appreciated being with him. He knew this because she had plenty of offers from other men to share her life with them, but she had kept very faithful to her connection with him.

He had not asked Marie to do this, but she had anyway. For Marie, it seemed that she had such high values. She had mentioned to him a number of times that every time she did go out with someone, their values clashed. She also decided, she said, that their relationship was more interesting to her. So, here was poor Marie just waiting for Darryl to decide to include her, even in a small way, in his life. Of course Marie had her own life and it was filled with people who loved her, but Marie had always made it clear to Darryl that their time together was the best time she had. She often said that she thought they had something special that she had never experienced with anyone else.

Darryl had to admit that this was the case for him too. In fact, he had once told Marie that it was a miracle that they had met in the first place. He shook his head. It was swimming with facts and his heart was erupting with lots of conflicting emotions. He felt guilty that he had waited so long to realize that, just like professional relationships, if you don't spend the right kind of time on the personal relationships that matter, sooner or later, they do change, grow weaker, or even die. He did not want to take that chance with Marie, but then again, how could he continue to live a life filled with challenge and still have Marie in his life?

It was as though Marie were reading his thoughts. "Darryl, just like you always say, you love a challenge. Even asking you this question has created a challenge for you. Don't you realize that there will never be a time in our relationship, professionally or if we choose, personally, that we won't have challenges?"

Darryl smiled at Marie and lifted her up into his lap and wrapped his arms around her. He knew that she was the best person in the world for him and that he had been crazy not to realize it sooner. "You mean you promise you will give me challenges every day so that I feel like I am alive?"

"Is that why you love a challenge?" asked Marie surprised. "I', very good at creating challenges for anyone or any situation. Of course, I can and would do that for you!"

They both laughed. "Well, then, I will give this conversation some very strong consideration."

Marie looked at Darryl and pulled on his ear in a teasing and yet firm way. "Listen, Darryl, you know we always promised that no matter what we would always have a relationship with our work and that we would also always be friends. I trust that you can take those very real commitments and realize that you have made them and kept them for the last two years, so perhaps you can just extend yourself a bit to include a more personal relationship that might benefit us both and even, perhaps, bring us lots of joy and adventure in our lives that we don't have now."

"Ok, ok!" Darryl smiled. He pulled Maried closer and hugged and kissed her passionately. "As you wish, my dear." With that, they Networlded happily ever after.

✳

*"When you wish upon a star..."*
*or something like that.*

# Epilogue

Once upon a time, not so long ago, there was a great adventure...

For Darryl and Marie, their great adventure took them into a Networld of ideas and actions, all of them surprising and rewarding and incredibly rich in texture and depth. It took them to small towns, to large cities, throughout America and abroad. They experienced the true power of relationships formed on common values.

They also experienced the rare find of friendship, camaraderie, and unique business opportunities. This adventure of Darryl and Marie's shows us that there are indeed modern day business fairytales that we can all share. All it takes is for us to look up from our desktop, palmtop, or day-planner and see the potential opportunities and relationships around us.

Are you like Darryl? Do you have a knack for developing relationships but no idea what to do with them? Are you like Marie? Do you wish to surround yourself with people of like-minded values but struggle to find them?

Are you experiencing a variety of 'takers' in your life and spending all your energies defending yourself or your department or your company? Are you like both Darryl and Marie who, in their personal career transitions, found a more passionate and powerful way of thriving in today's business world?

The Nanosecond Networlders teach us that there are solutions to some of the most compelling issues we face in our day-to-day lives and careers. These solutions start from the inside and only manifest themselves outward when we find people who can give us perspective from the outside in. These people become your partners and you theirs in your collective search for more effective ways to work and live. They are not afraid to tell you the truth, and that is supportive, not destructive. They are also prepared to receive your insight into their issues and are willing to accept the constructive truths that you can share with them.

Every decision is made in a split-second. We may deliberate for weeks or months on some, for minutes or hours on others, but the moment of commitment is always the moment that counts. The split-second decisions that Networlders make are different from decisions that others make. They are different in that they are firmly rooted in recognized values that help you see many paths towards seizing an opportunity. Networlders leverage the power of a boundaryless, value-based network of hundreds of inter-connecting circles of people; these circles are growing around the world and will continue to grow as more and more people decide to make those nano-second decisions to live their lives as Networlders.

Networlders make different and better decisions as they connect with people with shared-values forming circles both inside, outside, and across traditional company borders. There are no territorial disputes in Networlding. There is no information hoarding, no siege mentality, no blind watchmaker authority. Networlders recognize that the real adage today for doing business successfully is "He or she who shares the fastest, the best, and the most often, wins!" Networlding recognizes the naturally occurring organic interconnectedness of people from all walks of life and simply provides a fertile soil for those seeds of value-based relationships to be planted to create endless possibilities.

These possibilities are truly transformational. Think about that. Transformational. To transform means to change. Something cannot change beyond itself. An acorn cannot grow into a rose bush. Any individual acorn may have limitless potential and limitless 'possibilities' to become an oak tree, but only that. Its possibilities exist only within the limits of its inherent nature.

The wonderful thing about we who wrote this book and you who are reading it today is that we are human. And as humans, the limits our inherent nature contains are still far beyond our wildest dreams. We are capable of infinite possibilities to be the best we can be across the entire spectrum of human experience.

Personality is a choice. Success is a choice. And growth is a choice. Our growth comes from removing barriers from ourselves and realizing our true potential. No one can remove those barriers alone. Networlding shows us that through deep connections with others we can participate in an 'exchange' of ideas, values, support, and solutions to break through to our true potential – to realize our visions through our relationships.

What we the authors have tried to say within these covers, what we've hoped to convince you of, is that we need each other. We really do. For many years, business culture has been an uneasy truce between the 'lone ranger' entrepreneur and the government-like bureaucrat. Networlding creates a bridge for freeing people and organizations to reach their true potential by leveraging the limitless possibilities inherent in every conversation we have. That's exciting. That's new. That's a mighty oak of an idea, available to us all. We just have to look up for a split-second and connect.

So where could you go with Networlding? What are the possibilities in your life? In your company? What opportunities are you missing? Do you want to get started the way Marie and Darryl have? Who could you be including in your Networld?

✳

Will you start today? Do you have time to wait?

David R. Stover
And Melissa Giovagnoli
December 24, 2001
Chicago, IL

# "Once upon a time, not so long ago, there was a great adventure…"

That's how most fairytales start. Yet between these covers, Melissa Giovagnoli and David Stover have created a modern business fairy tale based on concepts that are rapidly becoming more critical to globally successful businesses today.

Do you have a knack for developing relationships but no idea what to do with them? Do you wish to surround yourself with people of like-minded values but struggle to find them? Are you experiencing a variety of 'takers' in your life, and spending all your energies defending yourself or your department or your company?

The Nanosecond Networlders show us that there are compelling new solutions to some of the most vexing cross-cultural, career, and organizational business issues we face today. These solutions recognize that every decision is made in a split-second, and that although we often deliberate for months, the moment of commitment is the moment that counts. Making that commitment in a way that is firmly rooted in recognized individual core values is the key.

Personal and career growth comes from removing barriers to realize our true potential. No one can remove those barriers alone. This book shows us how to participate in an 'exchange' of ideas, values, and solutions to break through to our true potential-by leveraging the limitless possibilities inherent in every conversation we have.

That's exciting. That's new. That's a mighty oak of an idea, available to us all.

**Networld Publishers**
**NETWORLDING**
*Books that inspire and change the world*

ISBN 0-9723467-0-8
$14.95 Canada
$11.95 US

6257713R0

Made in the USA
Charleston, SC
02 October 2010